T0113288

A MARINE'S PROMISE TO GOD

A MEMOIR OF VIETNAM

DAVID L. RAY

WESTBOW PRESS®
A DIVISION OF THOMAS NELSON & ZONDERVAN

WestBow Press books may be ordered through booksellers or by contacting:

WestBow Press
A Division of Thomas Nelson & Zondervan
1663 Liberty Drive
Bloomington, IN 47403
www.westbowpress.com
1 (866) 928-1240

ISBN: 978-1-5127-3628-1 (sc)
ISBN: 978-1-5127-3629-8 (e)

Library of Congress Control Number: 2016905322

Print information available on the last page.

WestBow Press rev. date: 4/4/2016

CONTENTS

Dedicated to the memory of my parents,
Bill and Ruth Ray.

YOU KNOW YOU'RE A MARINE GRUNT WHEN –

You have been wearing the same unlaundered clothes 24/7 for a couple of months.

You haven't slept in a bed for several months.

You haven't shaved for a few days -- and neither have the

You wash your clothes in the river while you're still wearing them.

Your boots have never seen polish

Your palms have nicotine stains from cupping your cigarette after dark.

You shave out of the steel pot of your helmet.

You use little balls of C-4 plastic explosive to heat your C-rations.

You keep 400 to 600 rounds (bullets) of ammunition with you.

Your closest companion 24/7 is your rifle.

You haven't had a cold drink in almost two months

Your pack and other gear you have to carry weighs as much as your older sister.

All they've given you to eat for a couple of months is C Rations and a can of Dinty Moore stew from home which is to die for.

You know it wasn't a straw that broke the camel's back it was a can of machine gun ammo.

The guys who have showers and beds to sleep in are at the Bob Hope show and you're still in the jungle.

The Summer of 69

I graduated from high school in 1967 and went to Northwest Missouri State University on a football scholarship. If I had not had the scholarship, I might have joined the military, because there was a part of me that wanted a piece of the Vietnam war. My friends and I had grown up in the shadow of our fathers and their participation in WW II, and I didn't feel that I should necessarily have it easy while my fellow Americans were fighting a war. But I loved football and with the scholarship, I chose to go to college.

I played two seasons of football but let my grade point drop below a C, so at the end of the fall semester of 1968, I got suspended from school for a semester. In those times the draft was "Johnny on the spot" and Uncle Sam was saying he wanted me. It looked like I was going to get a piece of that war after all.

I joined the Marines in mid May 1969 on the "90 day delay" plan, which meant I wouldn't have to go to boot camp until mid-August . It was my intent to live life to the fullest for those three months. I took every opportunity to have fun with friends and family, while working two jobs.

In August my brother Gary and I headed off to western Oklahoma to visit friends of ours, the Whitakers. Paul was the minister at a church on the Cheyenne Indian Reservation. Previously, he'd been our minister at the Martin City Baptist Church in the south suburbs of Kansas City, Missouri. Gary and I were there for a couple of days and then I headed out for San Antonio, Texas on my own, to get with some of my relatives on the Ray side of the family.

On the way to San Antonio it was over 110 degrees. Without air conditioning in the car I was using "4/80 air conditioning:" four windows down at 80 miles per hour. Once in San Antonio, I spent most of my time with my cousin Jim Ray who was the same age as me. We had some good times including some drag races. He had a Chevy Chevelle with a 396 CI engine and I had a 1965 Plymouth Belvedere with a 383 CI engine and a big Hurst floor shift. We were fairly evenly matched and I am not sure we ever declared which car was the best.

From there I headed out to New Mexico then north into Colorado where I went to the Royal Gorge. After that I went further north into Wyoming, then east to Scottsbluff, Nebraska. From there I went to Omaha and spent the night with one of my college football teammates, Dan Troshynski. We had some good laughs talking about our experiences together at Northwest Missouri State. The next day I headed home to spend a few days with my parents and other relatives and friends before heading to Marine boot camp.

During those three months I was trying to live life to the fullest. I knew in the back of my mind that this could be the last summer of my life. By the grace of God it wasn't, but for several Marine friends of mine, which I would meet over the next several months, the summer of 1969 would be their last summer to ever spend with family and friends.

The Promise

This book is a testimony to the power of prayer. To be a "grunt" (infantry) in the jungles of Vietnam with the Seventh Marines was a very dangerous proposition. To make matters even worse, I would be assigned the position of squad point man for about six months. While I was in Vietnam, there was some heavy duty praying going on by me, and back home there were the prayers of my mother and father--Ruth and Bill Ray--my brother and sisters, aunts and uncles, cousins, and fellow members of my home church, Martin City Baptist Church,. I learned many years later that members always brought me before the Lord when they met together on Wednesday nights for prayer meeting. I am a living testimony that God answered their prayers!

When you make promises to God, you should remember that God has known for all eternity exactly what you were going to do your entire life. To make a hollow promise to God is the promise made by a fool. But when I entered the Marine Corps, I made a promise to Him that if he would get me through my tour in Vietnam alive, I WOULD NEVER, EVER FORGET.

The following stories of my time in Vietnam are written first and foremost as a way of keeping that promise. They show how God protected me, not just once, but many times during my tour. They also show the camaraderie of men in combat, the heroic as well as the routine, the serious as well as the light-hearted. They show the brave side of military servicemen, and the foolish side. But they also show the reality that most of us went to Vietnam to serve our country and to help an ally in need. The media has not often showed the honorable side of being in the military during Vietnam. I hope in part to right that wrong.

One important note: The Marine Corps is a volunteer force. To join the Marines during the Vietnam War, especially in the mid to late sixties, was undisputable patriotism. This patriotism obviously includes the career Marines who chose to remain in the Corps. To all my friends, in for a short time or lifers, ***Semper Fi***, Marines!

Things Usually Happened Really Fast

We were on a two squad patrol. I was walking point for Alpha Squad, Third Platoon and Bravo Squad was parallel to us about 100 feet to our right flank. Bravo Squad was walking on a trail while we were out in the open in a dried up rice paddy. When the trail went into a wooded area, Bravo squad continued into the woods and we stayed parallel out in the open.

We had no idea that a group of about seven or eight Viet Cong (South Vietnamese Communist Terrorists--also called VC), all armed with AK-47 automatic rifles were in the wooded area. They spotted Bravo squad coming down the trail and decided to try and hook up with a larger group of VC., which meant cutting across the open area we were in, since they were totally unaware that we were there. All of a sudden, the group of VC came running out of the woods about 100 feet right in front of me. At that point, they were totally surprised to see us and likewise, the feeling was mutual. It turned into the "Gunfight at the OK Corral," a life-or-death conflict seeing who could shoot who the fastest. Well, this time the U.S. Marines dropped three of the enemy within the first 10 seconds, while the rest of them went running back into the woods and we sent as many bullets as we could chasing after them.

There was a larger group of VC in a wooded area about 200 to 300 feet out in front of us and to our left. About a minute after we shot the three right in front of us, a larger group opened up on us. Bullets were flying everywhere, and we could hear them pop as they went flying past. Out of the corner of my eye, I saw my friend nicknamed "Arkansas" hit the ground like a sack of feed and I figured he had been hit. We quickly dropped down behind a paddy dike for protection. We were all shooting like crazy and I was going through 20 round magazines like they were going out of style, even though I was shooting with my M-16 set to semi-automatic. There were some little bushes on the paddy dike, and bullets from the VC shooting at us would clip little branches off which would fall right in front of me. Bullets that were coming in lower were kicking up dirt right next to me and all I could do was put as many bullets in the air as possible headed back in their direction.

I don't know how long this went on, but I would guess 20 to 30 minutes. I had started out with 18 magazines of 20 rounds each or 360 rounds. Well, I was down to just one magazine left, and that made me pretty nervous. Luckily, everything had pretty much come to an end. We started checking around to see what our casualties were, and unbelievably, no one had been hit! In fact, the only one close to being wounded was "Arkansas," who had a bullet graze the tip of his nose.

When we checked out the three VC we had killed, one of their AK-47s had four notches carved into the stock. We didn't know if those were for killing South Vietnamese civilians during their acts of terrorism or for shooting U.S. soldiers and Marines. Needless to say, those VC wouldn't be shooting anyone ever again.

Since I had almost run out of ammo during the skirmish, when we got re-supplied, I anxiously grabbed a bunch more. I loaded magazine after magazine and put them into the pouches of the bandoliers until

I had 21 magazines in bandoliers and another 9 magazines in my flak jacket pockets for a total of 30 magazines or 600 rounds. In addition to being a Marine, I am also an Eagle Scout. I believe that you have to "Be Prepared." For all the action I saw in my time overseas, the only recurring dream I have about Vietnam in the years since the war is that I have run out of ammo and I'm scrounging everywhere to get more.

We received word a few days after this firefight that Marine Recon had been checking out the area after the firefight and found some shallow graves. There, they had found five dead VC, which they figured we had killed during that firefight and we weren't aware of it.

Fast Rewind About Two Months

A Marine Corps chartered commercial airplane loaded with Marines, including me, arrived in DaNang from Okinawa. It was early March, 1970, and among the planeload were a few of the guys I had gone all through training with, from boot camp to Infantry Training to Advanced Infantry Training. Bill Taylor from Montana was a good friend of mine. We used to go to Anaheim, California on weekend liberties, often sharing a motel room. There was also Lonnie Halvorsen from Chicago, Ed Lavoi from Louisiana, Doug Duncan from Oregon and Ken Lennox, though I can't remember where Ken was from.

That first night in DaNang, we were with a group of guys who had managed to make it a year in Vietnam without getting killed, and were headed home. Some had easy jobs that weren't too dangerous a lot of them had been "grunts" and had seen more than their share of action. All of us new guys to country would get assigned to units the next day. The guys who had just finished their year were telling us that the toughest units to be with were the Seventh Regiment or the Fifth Regiment of the First Marine Division. The next day, when we got unit assignments, we were all assigned to the Seventh Marines. They trucked us to a helicopter pad, where we got on a CH-46 helicopter and were flown to the Seventh Regiment headquarters at "LZ (Landing Zone) Baldy."

LZ Baldy was a large base camp about a mile in diameter, with a landing strip for cargo planes and choppers. It was surrounded by about 100 yards of strand after strand of concertina razor wire to thwart attacks. The buildings were framed in wooden shacks with tin roofs. There were bunkers and sand bagged fortresses everywhere, along with rocket trenches.

Taylor, Halvorsen, Duncan and I got assigned to the Third Battalion. Taylor went to Lima Company, Halvorsen and Duncan went to Kilo Company, and I was assigned to Mike Company. As we went our separate ways, we wished each other "good luck," not knowing if we would ever see each other again. We never did.

Welcome to Mike Company

Some of the other guys and I made our way to the Mike Company rear area there at LZ Baldy. The only people at the Mike Company area were guys with re-supply and some administrative personnel. The actual combat Marines of the company itself were out there in the jungle somewhere, which is where they basically lived most of the time.

We were outfitted with rifles, ammunition, grenades, helmets, packs, flak jackets, ponchos, poncho liners, canteens and shovels. In Okinawa they had taken all of our stateside uniforms and white underwear and given us camouflage jungle fatigues and green underwear. They stored away all of our uniforms and gear, to get on our return home. At Mike Company said to forget the green boxers because we would be wearing the same clothes unlaundered for a month or more and underwear was impractical.

The next morning we climbed aboard a CH-46 re-supply chopper and up, up and away we went, headed for the jungle and Mike Company. As we came circling in for a landing in an area that had been cleared for the choppers, I was wondering what all of this was going to be like. We touched down and as I stepped off, I stepped into a totally different world, the kind of world that most people can't even come close to imagining. The world of wearing the same clothes 24/7 for one or two months at a time. The world of sleeping on the ground for months at a time whether it was dry or in the mud. The world of never getting enough sleep. The world of jungle rot sores that never healed because they could never dry out due to sweat, rain and wading through rice paddies and streams. The world of so many mosquitoes you'd swear they could pick you up and carry you away. If all of this wasn't bad enough, there was the constant threat of being killed at any moment. It could come from being on a day patrol, a night patrol, or an ambush, being attacked in your company perimeter at night, mortar attacks, as well as the ever present booby traps.

Most booby traps were made from grenades with their delays minimized. Most of the grenades were our own American made that our enemies had gotten their hands on in whatever way possible, and the other grenades were their own Chi-com (Chinese communist) grenades. The American grenades could have the pin and spoon assembly unscrewed, exposing the fuse and blasting cap. They could cut the fuse length way down and re-attach the blasting cap and screw it back in place. Whenever they rigged it as a booby trap, when the spoon would fly, the delay was down to about one second rather than five or six. The really nasty booby traps were dud artillery rounds that they would rig with battery activation of the igniters.

CH-46 Helicopter

My Squad

I was assigned to Third Platoon, and then to Alpha Squad. Mike Company was generally about 120 men consisting of three platoons of riflemen and one platoon of mortar men. Each platoon of riflemen had three regular squads and one squad of M60 machine guns. Each squad had about ten men in it, when they were up to strength.

The entire company would pack up and move every day, then dig in to a new position wherever we had moved. The reason we moved each day was to make sure we never gave the enemy more than one day to plan an attack. When we dug in each day, we would set up a circular perimeter about 200 feet in diameter. The perimeter consisted of two man fighting holes which were about five feet long, two and one-half feet wide and about three to four feet deep, with the dirt piled in front of the hole. We would set Claymore mines out in front of our position. The Claymores were command detonated by a wire about 125 feet long back to our fighting holes. Other than the Claymores and trip flares, there wasn't anything between us and the enemy. When I got to Alpha Squad, it was being "rebuilt." The squad had been ambushed while on a night patrol and most of the members of the squad were wounded. The only guy from the original squad was Simpson from California, who was the point man. The new guys were Corporal Roden the Squad Leader, who was starting his second tour of duty and was from Chicago and Mike West, who had been with Mike Company about a month.

Mike was from Virginia and still lives there. He and I still keep in touch and we see each other at the Mike Company Reunions. Other guys in the squad were Rick Watts, our Squad Radioman who was from Hollywood, Florida; Brady from Boston; David Saint John from Michigan who is still a friend; William Wesley Wilkerson ("Tex") from Odessa, Texas; Roger Thompson, a farmer from Indiana; Sims from Texarkana, Arkansas, (we called him "Arkansas") and Atlas, whose real name I can't remember. One of the guys who re-joined the squad after recovering from wounds was Davis Burton from Chicago.

As I said before, the company would move their position every day, whether it was a mile or five miles, so that first day with them, I arrived when they were about to move out. Besides all the regular gear we had to "hump," (Marine slang for "carry") the squad leaders would also pass out some additional stuff for each of us to carry--things like mortar rounds, Claymore mines, pop-up flares, trip flares, C-4 plastic explosive, spare radio batteries, LAAW Rockets (Land Anti-Tank Assault Weapons) and the straw that would break any camel's back -- a can of machine gun ammo. We didn't each have to carry all of this, but even when the supplies were spread around, a Marine would end up with two or three of these things, a couple of days of C-rations, plus his regular gear and six canteens of water. It often ended up being 80 to 100 pounds worth of stuff, and carrying that around in that climate was tiring! When I got there in March, it was already hot and the temperature could get over 100 degrees Fahrenheit a lot of the time.

That first day, we were in the foothills of the Que Son Mountains and we moved about two miles to a new position. That night our squad got an assignment to go on an all-night ambush down the hill from the company perimeter. There was a light rain, and we moved down the hill in the thick underbrush about 100 away. Our mission was to be a buffer in case the enemy would try to sneak up on our main position. We went with a 50 percent watch all night long, meaning every other man was awake and the in-between guys would try to get some sleep until it was their turn. It was pretty miserable and we were lucky to get a couple of hours of sleep all night.

We moved again the next day and then dug new fighting holes. The digging was done with our shovels, otherwise known as "entrenching tools". Digging our holes gave us calloused hands and our skin was like leather.

My second night in the bush, we were sitting on the edge of our fighting holes at about dusk. One of the other squads headed into the jungle in front of us, to go on a night patrol. When they were about 200 yards out, they got in a firefight with some Viet Cong (VC). With all the shooting going on, some stray bullets came buzzing over us. Since I was a rookie and this was the first enemy shooting I had been exposed to, I wasn't sure what to do. I jumped into my fighting hole and grabbed **all** of my ammo and started stacking up the magazines to be prepared for a big fight in case they attacked us. Corporal Roden just looked at me and chuckled. After a while, the shooting stopped and everything died down. Nothing more happened that night.

At night in the company perimeter, we would split up the watch so that 25 percent of the guys were awake at all times. That meant every other two-man fighting hole would always have a person awake. We would start the watch at 10:00 p.m. and go to 6:00 a.m. A guy might get 6 hours of sleep – if he was lucky.

When we were on watch, we had to depend on our hearing to detect if the enemy was trying to sneak up on our position. If we heard suspicious sounds long enough, we would throw a grenade towards the sound, first yelling "Fire in the hole" before you chucked it. Grenades going off all night became a common sound and we reached a level where we could actually sleep through the noise, mainly because we were so tired. We wouldn't fire our rifles unless we were being shot at. When a rifle was fired, the muzzle flash would give away the location of the shooter. We got used to sleeping through grenades going off in the middle of the night but knew when the shooting started, the manure had hit the fan and it was time to grab our rifle and jump into our fighting hole, and have at it. We always slept with our rifles right next to us and always slept with our boots on, because nobody wanted to be running around in their bare feet in a night attack. It was tough to get any sleep because of the mosquitos eating you alive. We had insect repellent, but it was usually so hot, we would sweat it right off. The mosquitos could bite right through our clothes and when we were laying there trying to get some sleep, they would drive us crazy. We could pull our poncho over us and die of the heat, or we could leave the ponchos off and get eaten alive. It was miserable.

After I had been out in the bush for just less than three weeks, I celebrated my twenty-first birthday. I can remember sitting on the edge of my fighting hole, wondering what I would be doing if I was back home.

Not too long after that, I got word that my friend Bill Taylor had been killed in action with Lima Company. As I said earlier, Bill and I went all through boot camp, infantry training, and advanced infantry training together. We had spent many a weekend in Anaheim, Calif. sharing motel rooms and icing down beer in the bath tub. Then when we shipped out together to Vietnam he went to Lima Company and I went to Mike Company. He was killed in a night attack and was awarded the Silver Star for bravery, though I never did find out what Taylor did that earned him that medal. Good bye good friend. His location on the Vietnam War Memorial Wall is Panel 12W-Line 37. For those who don't know, there are over 58,000 names on The Wall. For some, they are just names. For those of us who lived it, they are more than friends; they are family.

William Taylor

We Had a Worthwhile Mission

Our enemy was the Viet Cong (VC), who were South Vietnamese citizens who favored being under communist rule, like their neighbors in North Vietnam. They basically were terrorists, much like what we have experienced in Iraq and Afghanistan. They not only set out to kill the Americans and the South Vietnamese military, but also to terrorize their own countrymen and neighbors. The numbers show that they assassinated 36,725 of their fellow citizens (Source: DAV Department of Iowa Newsletter--Winter 2009). When we were on patrols, I personally had instances of village leaders begging us to stay and protect them from the ruthless VC killers. The rest of our enemy was the North Vietnamese Army (NVA) that had invaded from the north. Honestly, they weren't quite as ruthless as the VC, and for the most part, had come down from the north to fight the Americans. Many of the NVA troops had been drafted and didn't have the same mindset as the VC.

Our mission was to protect the South Vietnamese civilians and to find and destroy the Communists. Back in 1965 and 1966 the Marines used different tactics than we did when I was there in 1970. Individual Companies would build small bases and stay there for periods of time and run patrols. When I got there, they had changed their tactics to a system where we moved every day and kept the enemy off balance. The Marines had been providing CUPP units (Combined Unit Pacification

Platoons), for years that consisted of a Marine Platoon that would live in a village and work with the locals to protect them from the Communist terrorists. The locals that worked with the Marines were teenage boys too young to be in the South Vietnamese Army.

To get a better idea of what the communists were capable of, do a Google search on "Massacre at Hue"

How I Got the Point Man Job

It was early April, 1970. We were in our company perimeter one morning when another squad out on patrol got into a firefight with a large group of VC, probably 15 or 20. They radioed back to the company and asked for reinforcements, so our squad was sent to help them out.

We set out to meet up with the other squad, but they were about a mile away, so it took us a while to get there. The shooting had stopped by the time we arrived and we were told the shots were coming from an area that had a couple of huts in which people were living. We swept abreast towards the huts, without anything happening. All the huts in this part of the country had shelter holes dug underneath them, that could hold several people. I took one of my grenades and started yelling down the hole, "Li Di!" which means, "Come here!" Nothing was happening, so I kept yelling it down the hole. I then took my grenade and pulled the pin and yelled it again. Finally, someone started up out of the hole. It was an old man, followed by his wife, their adult daughter and a couple of little kids. It scared the wits out of me to think how close I came to throwing the grenade down that hole.

We then headed back to our Mike Company perimeter, which again was almost a mile away. Simpson was walking point man and had his helmet tipped to the back of his head. He said that was because most booby traps had a little bit of a delay, so it was protecting his backside. Corporal Roden was right behind Simpson and Rick Watts was carrying the radio right behind Corporal Roden.

As we were walking along a foot trail, all of a sudden I saw Simpson take off with a couple of running steps, then BOOM. He had felt his foot connect with a trip wire from a booby trap and he tried to outrun the explosion. He didn't make it and he got hit with shrapnel in the back. His helmet tipped back had worked for his neck and head, and his flak jacket took care of his back, but he caught shrapnel in the back of his legs. Also hit was Corporal Roden and Rick Watts. Nobody had any potentially fatal wounds.

We called in a Medevac for the three of them. Simpson only had a couple of months left on his one year tour, so he would be headed home. Corporal Roden would be getting his third Purple Heart, so he was headed home as well, and Rick Watts would go to Japan to get patched up and would be back in a few weeks.

Simpson was a real character. He used to sing a version of a popular song from 1966 called "Sweet Pea" by Tommy Roe. It went: "Oh, Sweet Pea, C'mon and dance with me. C'mon, c'mon, c'mon and dance with me."

His version was "Oh VC". In fact, while we were waiting for the medevac chopper to come in, and we had bandaged Simpson's wounds, he was laying on the ground singing it. He was in a good mood, since he knew his wounds would be sending him home.

His words to the song were:

> "Oh, VC, why you shoot at me? Why, oh why, oh why you shoot at me?
> I went to a firefight the other night. All the VC there were out of sight.
> Oh, VC, why you shoot at me? Why, oh why, oh why you shoot at me?"

The medevac chopper came in and before we loaded the three of them on it, Corporal Roden told Mike West to take over as Squad Leader. We got them loaded onto the chopper and away they went. Mike turned to me and said "Ray, take point". So there you have it. Just like that, I was the new point man for most of the next six months. I tilted my helmet to the back of my head and headed out, with the rest of the squad following me.

Each squad had a point man and there were three squads per platoon and three platoons in the Company. Therefore, there were nine point men per each company. Every time a squad was on a patrol or ambush, they had their point man take the lead. Whenever the entire company was moving to a new position each day, one of the squads would be the lead squad and their point man would be at the head of the entire company. The point man would have a shadow who would walk two or three steps behind him. The point would look for booby traps and straight down the trail and the shadow would look to the right and left for the enemy. I don't want to brag, but it took nerves of steel.

Needless to say, my prayers increased in volume and frequency after I became the squad point man. To be a point man in 1970 Vietnam with the Seventh Marines could possibly be the most dangerous job in the entire U.S. Military. I promised God that if he would get me through all of this, I WOULD NEVER EVER FORGET.

Atlas Gets Hit

Here comes some Guardian Angel help.

It wasn't too long after I became the Alpha squad point man, when we were on a patrol and all of a sudden "BOOM" came a report from back behind me. Atlas was about four or five men to the rear, when he walked around a bush on the opposite side of the trail than what I had led, and he hit a grenade booby trap.

He hadn't been fatally hit, but the concussion had broken both of his legs, leaving the bones sticking out. He had also caught some shrapnel in rear end, and because of all his wounds, he was in a lot of pain.

The Corpsman patched him up as well as he could, and we called in a medevac chopper. We then loaded him onto the chopper and that was the last time I ever saw him. I assume that after the medical personnel got him stabilized, they sent him to Japan for further medical treatment, then eventually back to the U.S.

When the Marines did a medevac, the main chopper that came in was a CH-46 double prop machine. Two Huey Cobra helicopters would also circle around the area for support, if needed. The Cobras were armed with rockets and automatic M79 grenade guns and could dish out a lot of firepower.

My First Look at Enemy Dead before the Story at the Beginning of this Book

My first look at a dead enemy combatant was my second day in the bush, when we walked past what was left of an enemy corpse along a foot trail. There was an encounter about a week after I had joined Mike Company in the bush, when "Chief," as we knew him--who was part Indian--killed an NVA officer when they were out on patrol. Chief got the officer's 9 mm pistol, but anyone not on the patrol never saw the body.

It was about my third or fourth week in the bush, when the company was in their perimeter, Bravo squad from our platoon was on a patrol, and we heard them get into a firefight. They radioed back that they had killed three VC, so our Platoon Commander, Lieutenant Gosier asked if they could bring back the bodies. They said they could, and a while later they returned with the three VC hanging from poles with their hands and feet tied together.

An M-16 rifle bullet can do some pretty terrible things to the human body. One of the VC had been hit in the head, and it blew the top of his head off and his brains had been blown out, with just an empty cavity left.

It doesn't settle too well, knowing that this can happen to you as well .I can't remember if it was this same day or a day or two later when we were in our company perimeter and could hear a thump, thump, thumping sound. Within a few seconds, we all realized that the thumping was the VC shooting a bunch of mortar rounds. We kind of looked at each other then in an instant, everybody was running for their fighting holes. We all jumped in our two-man holes, but that day, the VC were pretty inaccurate and the mortar rounds missed us by at least 100 feet. The sound from where the mortars had been fired was maybe 500 yards away, back in the jungle. We all opened up with rifle and machine gun fire for a while, but I am sure they were long gone by then. We wondered if the VC were trying to get some payback for their comrades we had just killed.

Rick Watts and Me

Rick had been wounded when Simpson hit the booby trap, and was sent to Japan for medical care. He was back again in three or four weeks and we became good friends. Rick was the squad radioman and he and I would dig our two-man fighting holes together.

Rick being from Hollywood, Florida, and me being from the south edge of Kansas City, Missouri, we would sit around and talk about things back. He would brag about his "chopper" motorcycle and I would brag about my '65 Plymouth with a 383 engine and a big Hurst four-speed shifter. We decided that when we were back home again, I would come pay him a visit in Florida and we would have some wild times.

One time when we had humped down out of the Que Son Mountains and the company dug in on one of the foothills, Rick and I were digging a fighting hole in ground as hard as a rock. We probably only got it dug about 18 inches deep, when we said "Oh well!" and decided that would have to do.

It was hot as blazes that day, so I attached my bayonet to my rifle, stuck it in the ground and tied one end of my poncho liner to it on the sling swivel and the other end to a bush to make a little shade. It wasn't too long after that, that we started taking on some enemy rifle fire out in front of our perimeter. Everybody was grabbing their rifles and scrambling for their holes. I was trying to get the poncho liner untied from my rifle's sling swivel, and couldn't get it undone .So I just grabbed my rifle and headed for the hole, dragging the poncho liner behind me. Rick looked at me and just busted out laughing. Then the two of us squeezed into our sorry excuse for a fighting hole, with most of our bodies exposed and then he laughed just that much harder. While he was still laughing, he said, "This stupid hole wouldn't make a decent latrine!"

Rick liked to pull pranks on the guys in our squad. Something he did two or three times, was if somebody had left their cigarette pack laying somewhere unattended and had gone to do something else, Rick would pick a cigarette out of the pack. He would then pick some of the tobacco out of it and pour some gun powder in from an M-16 round, then put some tobacco back to make it look normal. When whoever the cigarettes belonged to would light up, we would wait with anticipation to see if that was the loaded cigarette. If it was, within a few seconds, it would flash and poof when he reached the gun powder, and we would all laugh our butts off, except the victim.

Our First KIA's (Killed in Action) After I Joined Mike Company

A little while after I became squad point man, Corporal Busby became our Squad Leader. Mike West was still with the squad, but Busby would be our Squad Leader for a while.

It was April 22, 1970 and our company perimeter was set in on top of a foot hill of the Que Son Mountains. Our squad was on patrol down at the base of the foothills and another squad from First Platoon was on patrol going up a foot trail on one of the adjacent foot hills. Suddenly, the other patrol broke into a big firefight.

What had happened, was as the other squad was going up the hill on the foot trail, they heard the enemy coming up behind them, talking to each other unaware of the Marine patrol in front of them. The Marine patrol quickly set up an ambush and sprang it as the VC came up the trail. They shot several of the VC and after everything died down, they went down the trail to check on the enemy soldiers they had just shot. But when they got to the bodies of the enemy, the rest of the VC who had not gone away then ambushed the Marines. The fighting went on sporadically for a while and when things died down, they called in medevac choppers.

It was getting late in the afternoon, and as the choppers tried to evacuate them in the thick jungle they had to hover above and drop cables down to try and lift out the dead and wounded. The VC were still around and were shooting at the choppers, so they would have to peel off for a time and get out of range of the rifle fire. This went on a few times, and soon the sun set. We then had to call in aircraft illumination, which entails a cargo plane dropping huge illumination canisters- which would float down by parachute and light up the sky for the evacuation. Our helicopters tried several times to get to our position and kept getting enemy fire. It took half the night, but they finally got everybody out. At the end of it all, two Marines were killed in the fight and two more died of their wounds in the next couple of days. I didn't know them personally, but knew their faces. When some 120 guys live together 24 hours a day, 7 days a week, you at least recognize everyone's faces, even if you don't know their names.

I have since found out who they were. Below are their names and location on the Vietnam Memorial Wall:

Don Scott- Panel 11 W Line 38, Navy Corpsman
Thomas McKinney, Panel 11 W Line 38
Joseph Pogue- Panel 11 W Line 42
David Ellefson - Panel 11 W Line 49
Semper Fi, Marines!

The Story at the Beginning of this Book

It wasn't too much longer after that April firefight, that the story I gave at the beginning of this book took place when we were on the two squad patrol. My Guardian Angel was definitely at work that day. When the VC came running out in front of us, with me at the front, it was an "equal opportunity" shootout. There were several of them with their AK-47 rifles and really only three or four of us in a position close enough to them to do any shooting. We generally kept a 20 to 30 foot space between us, while on patrol, so just "me and my shadow" and a couple of others were in a position to shoot. It could have turned out the other way, with some of my friends and me lying dead on the ground, but by the grace of God and some Marine Corps skill it turned out the way it did.

That first encounter was enough to make any Guardian Angel feel they had done a day's work, but that wasn't the end of the day yet. The VC's friends out across an open dried up rice paddy opened up on us, and that's when the shooting really got going. As I said at the beginning, we ducked behind a rice paddy dike, which had some small bushes on it, and the bullets were so thick, that little twigs were getting clipped off and falling next to me. Bullets were also kicking up dirt on the paddy dike next to me. I could hear the bullets go by. The ones that were 20 or 30 feet away would make a fast "whishing" sound, the ones that were closer, would make more of a popping noise. Needless to say, you would never hear the one that hit you.

When the shooting had stopped, we were given orders to form a wedge with the two squads and head out across the open area towards where all the enemy fire had come from. I'm not sure if that order came over the radio from our Platoon Commander or the Company Commander. All I know is that it didn't seem like a good idea, especially when they had me at the lead of the wedge. If any of the enemy was still there, the rest of the guys and I were prime targets. We lucked out and they were all gone and for the time being at least, I wasn't a shooting gallery target.

I thanked God for his protection and again told him that if He would get me through all of this, I WOULD NEVER EVER FORGET.

When I Started Smoking

At this time, we were in the flatlands at the base of the mountains. The area where we were digging in was a fairly open area without many bushes or trees. Our Company Commander didn't want us to put our ponchos together and make pup tents, because he thought a little moon-light would make us silhouette them at night and we'd become targets for the enemy. It was raining that evening and it rained all night long. All we could do was pull our ponchos over us and lay there in the rainwater all night.

The next morning when I got up soaking wet and miserable, I was looking at what was left of my C-rations. All of the food was gone since we hadn't been resupplied. All that was left was the accessory pack, which was a small foil pouch that had instant coffee, creamer, sugar, toilet paper, a plastic spoon and a small four-pack of cigarettes. I had always given my cigarettes to one of the guys that smoked, but that morning I needed something, so I lit up a cigarette and thus became a smoker. It really tasted good, even if it was a 20 year-old Lucky Strike. I didn't smoke much after I got out of the Marines and totally quit about 12 years ago.

Firebase Bushwhack

One day the whole company was flown to the top of a mountain to an artillery base called Firebase Bushwhack. We were to be the guards of the base in case of attack. We'd be there for a week, but for us, that was like getting a week's vacation. For that week, we would be in the one location and not have to move our position every day and not have to dig a new fighting hole. We wouldn't have to run daytime or nighttime patrols and for the most part we could just goof off and stand watch all day and take turns standing watch at night. We were actually given some really crude living quarters which were small, two man huts built from ammo boxes filled with dirt and stacked on top of each other about four feet high, They then had a piece of plywood for a roof. Compared to our usual accommodations, this was like staying at the Hilton!

The craziest thing happened one day while we were there. All the trash from the firebase was thrown down the side of the mountain, where it would pile up about 100 feet down the slope. Whenever it accumulated to a sizeable heap, someone would throw a trip flare down into the trash pile to burn it. One day while a pile of trash was burning, a re-supply chopper was coming in with a net hanging below it, filled with artillery rounds and a 55 gallon drum of gasoline for the jeep on the base. I guess a down draft hit the chopper and the hook holding the net came loose and the whole thing fell into the trash fire. Somebody yelled "Get up the hill! Get up the hill!" and as I scrambled to get out of the way, the drum of gasoline exploded, heating up my backside.

We all had to move over to the other side of the mountain and get into bunkers, because the artillery rounds got hot enough that they began to "cook off" getting hot enough to explode. Shrapnel would go buzzing through the air and we had to hide out in the bunkers until enough time had gone by that we felt confident that no more rounds were going to explode.

When the officers let us crawl out of the bunkers, the guys from our squad and I went back over to the other side of the mountain, where our makeshift huts had been. Three of the huts had been totally destroyed, including mine. My pack had been in there, along with my pictures from home and some C-rations. Oh, well! I had to write home for new pictures.

Like I said, we were there for a week, then it was back to the usual routine of moving every day, digging a new fighting hole every day, and going on daytime and night patrols.

Time to do Some Laundry

Wearing the same clothes for one to two months at a time produced some real smelly Marines. We got used to it because - what else could we do? Sometimes we would get a break, and if the whole company was moving to a new position and we came across a river, then the Company Commander would let us clean up a bit. Half the company would surround a part of the river and act as security for the other half who would get in the river and clean up and vice-versa. First we would do our laundry, while wearing it then we would take off our clothes and take a bath.

On one occasion our platoon was part of the security and we were spreading out to surround part of the river while another platoon washed up, just then Davis Burton of our squad hit a grenade booby trap. I went running over to help him and was the first guy to get to him. He was alive and didn't appear to be critically wounded. He had caught three or four pieces of shrapnel in his legs and one had hit his knee where clear fluid was coming out. Needless to say, he had plenty of bleeding going on, too. We got him bandaged up and loaded onto a medevac chopper and that was the last we saw of him. This was his ticket home, which happened to be Chicago. It was going to be Davis' second Purple Heart. He had been wounded the first time when the squad was ambushed before I got to Mike Company.

Battalion Operation

If you have Google Earth and want to see exactly where this was taking place, do a "fly to" search by putting the coordinates in exactly like this: 15 44' 04.25" N, 108 09' 57.40" E then hit the ENTER Key. It will fly to Hill 848 and you will be looking straight down on it, so to get a look at the terrain put the mouse arrow in the middle of the screen and do a quick left click. Then hold the Shift key with your left hand and hit the down arrow with your right, and it should give you a lower angle of the mountains.

It was May 27, 1970 and the Third Battalion of Seventh Marines was headed for Hill 848 in the Que Son Mountains. The 848 was the number on the old French relief maps that designated the altitude in meters at the highest point of each mountain. The base of the hill was about 100 feet in altitude, which means that from the bottom of the hill to the top was about 2,500 feet in altitude.

The Marines and Navy were pounding the top of the hill with 500 lb. bombs from F-4 Phantom fighter jets. They basically were blowing away all the trees to allow us to land in CH-46 and CH-53 helicopters. Chopper after chopper was unloading Mike Company and the rest of the battalion on top of the hill. Little did I know that this day was going to require some Divine protection a couple of times.

Mike Company was told to take the lead on a mountain foot trail along the ridgeline of the mountains. Our squad was called up to the front and told to take point, which meant I was going to be point man for the entire battalion. What a privilege! (I say that with a certain amount of sarcasm).

Now about that time, I got a real break, as the "powers that be" sent a scout dog and his handler up to the front to walk point with me. This was the first and only time we ever had scout dogs help walk point.

As it turns out, there was a "Kit Carson Scout" giving directions from several men behind me, relating to how to get to some caves where an NVA hospital was. A "Kit Carson Scout" was a former Viet Cong who had come over to our side and could be rewarded with money if he led us to caches of weapons and supplies.

As we went down the trail, the dog trotted along in front of us, until he was about 50 or 75 feet ahead, then he would trot back to the dog handler and me. The dog handler would give him a reassuring pat on the head and he would turn around and go back down the trail as we kept moving forward.

The dog was about 75 feet in front of us when he stopped and looked into the jungle to the right side. He then growled and leaped, and as he leaped a shot rang out. I started firing like crazy toward where the shot came from. When things settled down I slowly made my way to the dog. He had been wounded and the enemy sniper had gotten away. There is a picture of this dog and his handler on page 120 of the Time Life series on the Vietnam War in the Volume titled "Combat Photographer" the dog handler's name was Isaiah Martin. The photo was dated May 30 and because of that, that's the date I went by for years until I was able to determine our action occurred on May 27th.

We called in a medevac chopper for the dog and he and his handler got on and we proceeded down the trail. Like I said, that was the first and only time we had a scout dog. If he hadn't been ahead of us, "you know who" would have been in that sniper's sights. That bullet had my name on it.

It wasn't until just recently I was able to determine the date was May 27th Exactly three years later, I would marry Renee, my bride of more than forty years now and exactly three years after that, our son Aaron was born.

Another scout dog and handler were called up to walk point with me. This handler was wearing black, rather than the typical Marine Corps camouflage. We were told by the Kit Carson Scout to take a trail down along the side of Hill 845. As we made our way along that trail, we received instructions to take another trail that led to the caves. All of Mike Company headed for the caves while the next company behind us continued on the other trail taking the dog and handler with them. Within about an hour or so, that dog handler was hit with a sniper's bullet. It was a pretty complicated medevac in the triple canopy jungle and he died before they could get him out. His name was Robert Rhodes. His location on the Vietnam War Memorial Wall is Panel 10W Line 110.

We went down the trail to the caves. Actually most of it consisted of big rock overhangs and not enclosed caves like you might think. The NVA had very recently left and they had a pot of tea over some coals and the tea was still hot. We were basically checking out the area for anything we could find. After a while a shot rang out down in an actual cave. It was our Platoon Sergeant, Grady Eiland, who had been exploring down in a cave. Our Platoon Commander Lieutenant Gosier yelled down into the cave and asked what was going on. Sergeant Eiland yelled back that he had heard something and he psyched out and took a shot with his 45 pistol. Lieutenant Gosier didn't want his Platoon Sergeant scrounging around down in a cave and ordered him out. When he came out, the Lieutenant asked for volunteers to go back into the cave and find out what was down there. Like an idiot, I volunteered.

I borrowed a 45 pistol from someone and got the flashlight from Sergeant Eiland and then proceeded down into the cave. Roger Thompson followed behind me as well as some of the other guys from our squad.

The cave went almost straight down for about eight feet or so, then went to the right. It was about five and one-half feet high, so I had to bend over. It was about six feet wide and went about six or eight feet and made a sharp bend to the left. There was a trickle of a stream running on the floor of the cave coming from an opening that was about 10 by 10 inches. I got down on the floor of the cave and shined the flashlight into that opening. The little tunnel went back about six or eight feet and the flashlight shined on what was the thigh of a NVA wearing shorts. I could see his skin and knew it was a person. I began yelling at him to "*Chu Hoi*," which was supposed to be a program we had been told to yell at enemy combatants as a signal for them to surrender. I didn't know at the time that *chu hoi* really meant "brotherhood" and not "surrender" and I was yelling obscenities at him along with *chu hoi* .So I thought I was yelling, "Surrender!" and in reality I was yelling, "Brotherhood" in a real nasty tone.

Nothing was happening so I aimed in and squeezed off a shot with the 45. Blood started running down with the water trickling from the stream on the cave floor. I yelled at him some more with no result, so I squeezed off another shot. Still nothing .I then realized I was going to have to go around the bend of the cave and go after him. I started around the sharp bend to the left, then it made a sharp bend to the right. I was holding the 45 in my right hand with my finger right on the trigger and had the flashlight in my left hand, when suddenly I saw something moving and fired off another shot. This enemy soldier is now yelling, "Chu hoi! Chu hoi!" I shined the flashlight on him, and he was not the same guy I had shot just a few moments ago. I had hit this one in the hip and he had his hands up to surrender. I motioned for him to come out so he limped towards me and I pushed him past me to Roger Thompson. Lo and behold, there were three more of them back there, including the guy I had already put two bullets in. As I was getting the rest of them out of there, and was looking around, I found they had rifles and grenades back in the area they were evacuating. These guys, if they wanted to be heroes and go out in a blaze of glory, could have chucked a grenade at me and that would have been the end of yours truly. Thankfully they weren't that brave and I am still here to tell the story. My Guardian Angel was still on the job.

We sent the prisoners out of the cave, helping the wounded ones. The same photographer who got the picture of the wounded dog also got a picture of the wounded NVA being helped out of the cave by David Saint John. I didn't know it until about 30 years later but that picture was published in **Stars and Stripes**, a magazine for the U.S. Armed Forces. David has a copy of the magazine and showed it to me about 10 years ago.

We had a new squad leader at this time--a career Marine named J.C. Hines-- who was on his second tour in Vietnam. As we were passing the rifles and grenades up out of the cave, he latched on to a Chinese rifle-- the SKS, which is not full automatic and was alright to keep as a souvenir.

It was now getting late in the day, and it was starting to get dark, so we didn't call in a medevac for the wounded NVA and would do it the next day in full daylight. Our squad guarded the four NVA we'd captured all night. At first, they were scared to death of us. They had heard bad things about Americans in general and even worse things about the Marines. They were nearly overjoyed to find that we weren't as terrible as they had been told as long as they weren't in combat against us.

A couple days later I thought back about my recent experience and decided I probably wouldn't volunteer for cave duty again. I thanked the Lord for his protection, and I knew the prayers were coming big time from back home, too. My mother has told me many times of how she would wake up in the middle of the night and sit straight up in bed and start praying. The middle of the night in Kansas City is the middle of the day in Vietnam and quite often, that was when I needed the prayers for immediate protection. I was praying too, but as I said, I told God that if he would get me through this I WOULD NEVER, EVERFORGET.

A Letter to Home

My father saved all my letters I sent home and after he died in 1996 my mother gave them to me. The following is a transcript of one of them:

June 5th

Hi Everyone,

Things here are awful hot right now, and all we think about are things that are cool. We're still on our battalion operation is why I haven't had time to write sooner. We're not in the Que Son Mountains anymore, but now we've moved down into the Que Son Valley. They think that all the N.V.A. got scared and headed down here in the valley. I found out that because of that deal with the enemy in the cave that I'll probably get a promotion and some other kind of recognition.

I've used up all that film you sent me, and as soon as we go back to the rear again I'll mail it home.

I'm sending another check home with this so take my tithe out and bank the rest of it.

I don't know what you've found out about my driver's license, but when I do get back, I'll be needing one, so please see what you can do.

If you send anymore packages, I'd appreciate it if you could put some Flying Dutchman pipe tobacco in it. The only pipe tobacco we get around here is cherry blend, and I'm pretty tired of it, besides Flying Dutchman is about the best tobacco around.

The way things are looking now, we won't get pulled until around August or September. Be sure and save some home grown food so I can really chow down when I get back. I'm pretty sure that because I'm a bush Marine that I'll get discharged upon arriving in the states, so I may just end up being in this Green Machine only 12 or 13 months. It will sure be nice to be a free man again.

Everyone out here in the bush are getting pretty hacked off because we haven't had a rehab in almost 40 days, and we're beginning to turn into animals. The word is that we're supposed to go on stack arms again either at the end of this month or early July.

I'm pretty sure I'm going to buy another car when I get back, and I'm thinking in the line of a '69 GTX.

When I think of coming home in time for fall, it really psyches me up. That's my favorite time of the year, and I'll probably be the happiest guy in the world.

You've asked if we keep up with the world news. Well, we do, most of the time we get to have radios out here, and listen to them in the daytime only. They have a real good American station that we can listen to, and keep up with the news.

Well, I don't have anything more to say for now, just keep the mail coming, and I'll be seeing you before you know it.

David

The Rope Bridge

My Guardian Angel was called back on duty again

A couple of weeks after the battalion operation, we were back down in the flatlands and were on a two squad patrol. I was leading the way when we came upon a rope bridge crossing a swiftly moving stream. I went ahead and crossed over the rope bridge, with our squad and the other squad following me. On the other side of the bridge, our two squads split up and went on separate patrols.

While out on our patrols, I don't remember anything happening that was noteworthy, and as we communicated with each other, we planned on meeting up again at the rope bridge. When we met there, the other squad said they would cross it first, since we had led the way across the first time. I thought that was fine with me, so they started across the bridge. A sniper started firing at them and killed one of their squad members. I can't remember if it was the point man or not, but I think it was. Again, I had had some divine protection. I don't know what would have happened if I had walked point across that rope bridge for the second time that day, and only God knows for sure.

Needless to say, the rest of us weren't going across that rope bridge, so we crossed that swift moving stream by wading across. It was about three feet deep and took everything we could muster to ford it and keep from being swept away. We made it across, but had lost another member of Mike Company that day.

Ken Martin Panel 9W Line 56

Picnic Anyone?

We were on a two day rest at our Battalion headquarters on LZ Baldy and had finally been able to get some clean clothes. Late in the afternoon some of the guys from our platoon went to a small hut belonging to the Seabees, that they called "The Pig" where they would sell us beer. Earlier, the Sea Bees had a wiener roast and had also made some potato salad and baked beans. The leftovers were still sitting on a table outside the hut. This seemed too good to pass up, so we decided to have some of the goodies with our beer and served up some onto paper plates. Some wise guy decided to throw one of the full plates at someone else, and soon it broke into an all-out food fight. What a mess! We all ended up with potato salad and baked beans all over our clean clothes and in our hair. We weren't going to be getting any clean clothes and there weren't any showers to clean off, either, so we all smelled like a big picnic.

Soon someone from our company came looking for us and informed us that Recon had spotted a battalion sized unit of NVA heading in the direction of LZ Baldy. It was time to get back and get our fighting gear and head to the fighting holes on the perimeter. Most of us grabbed some beers to take along and then went rushing back to our company area to get our rifles, ammunition, helmets and flak jackets and then started for the fighting holes. About then, our Platoon Commander saw most of us with a couple of beers apiece in our hands and he just shook his head.

When we manned the fighting holes and were sipping our beer, we thought it was a real bite that and were pretty aggravated that these stupid NVA were interrupting the good time we had been having at "The Pig." So while we manned our fighting holes and drank our beer, a couple of guys looked out over all the razor wire, in the direction from which the enemy might be coming, and started yelling, "Come on you lousy Communists! Come ahead and attack us." After all that, nothing happened, but we had to stay there half the night just in case.

Fourth of July Celebrating

I think it was during this last stay at LZ Baldy, when I was trying to get a case of trench foot cured. I stayed behind for a couple of days while the rest of Mike Company went back to the jungle. I had to be on guard duty at night and was there the night of July 3rd. We had been given instructions, that when midnight came and it was the Fourth of July, there weren't to be any celebrations.

I was sitting on the edge of my fighting hole at midnight and it became the Fourth of July. I heard a grenade go off about 200 feet off to my right, then someone sprayed the sky with tracer, and it was "Katie bar the Door! I joined in with everyone else and started throwing grenades, shooting pop up flares, and spraying tracers into the sky. Then the big eight inch cannons got in on the action. You have never heard any fireworks in your life that compare to a volley of 8--inch bore cannons going off! They had zeroed in on a small mountain a few miles away and were just cutting loose with a tremendously loud noise. Things finally settled down after a while, but we were all psyched up by the celebration we had just had for our country's birthday.

That morning, nobody got in trouble for the fireworks.

The Guys in Our Squad and Platoon

Since the time I had joined Mike Company, five men had been wounded from our squad. One of which had returned, that being Rick Watts. I have already given some information about Rick and his background here's some more about the rest of the guys.

Our Squad Leader at this time was J.C. Hines. He was a career Marine and this was his second tour of Vietnam. He was from upstate New York, and he always made sure you knew that he wasn't from New York City, and that upstate was more like Vermont J.C. was married and had a little boy. He was a real good Marine and good Squad Leader.

Mike West was from the Roanoke, Virginia area, made it home safely, and still lives in Virginia. He and I stay in touch with each other and got together about 20 years ago in Illinois. We both made it to a reunion in 2009 for Mike Company in Columbus, Ohio. It's always good getting to see old friends.

David St. John was from Michigan and he still lives there and we have kept in touch with each other, too. David and I got together in Chicago several years ago and he was also at the 2009 Mike Company reunion in Ohio. David is the son of a Baptist Minister and in Vietnam he somehow seemed like a preacher's son, in that his language was not as bad as most Marines and he didn't smoke while I knew him. He did, however, start smoking sometime after that.

Brady was from Boston and I never even knew his first name. He had a typical Bostonian accent, and I got a kick out of just listening to him talk. He had been with the Third Marine Division when they were pulled out of Vietnam and was reassigned to Mike Company. He was with Alpha Squad when I was assigned to it and I would love to get in touch with him, but how do you find a guy named Brady in Boston?

Sims was from Texarkana, Arkansas, so we just called him "Arkansas." I never knew his first name either. I figured it wouldn't be very easy to find him, and I haven't seen or talked to him since Vietnam.

Roger Thompson had grown up on a farm in Indiana. He would tell about going out to the smokehouse where they were smoking some hams and taking a knife and cutting off a piece and taking some tasty bites. All of us would tell food stories and torture ourselves. I remember Roger had a girlfriend that wrote him a "Dear John" while we were together, and it really got to him. Guess what, I had a girlfriend I had met in Anaheim, California on a weekend leave. She wrote me a "Dear John" letter, too, but I was too preoccupied with just surviving to worry about it.

William Wesley Wilkerson was from Odessa, Texas and we just called him "Tex." He was married and had a little boy back home. Tex was the only Marine that I ever met that had been drafted. When we were in Vietnam, He seemed like a natural to be a Marine. I phoned him about 1990 to reconnect, and he seemed like he couldn't care less that I had called. I haven't called him since.

One of the Corpsmen in our platoon was Lonnie Johnson, who ended up becoming a Baptist minister. He was at the Mike Company reunion in Branson, Missouri in 2000, and I found out he was the pastor at Ruskin Heights Baptist Church in a suburb of Kansas City. Since my wife and I would visit KC fairly often, we would get together with Lonnie and his wife on occasion. Eventually, he moved to California and then to South Dakota, but we still stay in touch.

Layne Smith was from Georgia and was in the Third Platoon Machine Gun Squad. Layne was also at the 2000 Mike Company reunion in Branson and also at the 2009 reunion in Columbus. He's one of the faithful that has been going to all of them since 2000. Layne and I email and call each other from time to time.

Also in the Third Platoon Machine Gun Squad were "Music" from Tennessee, Curt Colyear from California and Orr from Kansas. Since I was from Kansas City, I considered that I had "dual citizenship" for both Missouri and Kansas, so Orr was my "homey."

Ron Phroper in Bravo Squad was from St. Joseph, Missouri, so he was another "homey." I have seen Ron a couple of times since Vietnam. Another friend from Bravo Squad was Ernest "Mac" Barber from Alabama. He would always give me a bunch of guff about being a Yankee and I would hassle him about the country music he liked. A lot of guys from the South liked country music, and while there were plenty of people in Kansas City that liked country, I preferred rock (and still do).

"Curly's" real name was Smitty Victoria, and he was from Mississippi. I can't tell you a lot about him and I'm not even sure where he ended up. A couple of other guys in our squad I can't recall much about were Woods and "Cowboy." Woods was from New York City and was pretty quiet. Cowboy was from somewhere in Texas and I don't even know his real name. He was medevacked out for heat exhaustion, and we never saw him again.

Our Platoon Commander was Lieutenant Gosier. He was from upstate New York like J.C. Hines, so they hit it off pretty good. I never spent time just shooting the breeze with him, so I didn't know a lot about him.

Our Platoon Sergeant was Grady Eiland from Alabama. He was a career Marine, and this was his second tour of duty. He was engaged to a woman Marine. He was a very good Marine and when he would go on patrols with our squad, he would generally walk Shadow for me.

Our Company Commander was Lt. McAdams who was a tall guy with a big dark moustache. Two of the earlier Company Commanders through the years ended up becoming Generals. General Draude and General Van Ripper.

Front to back is Lt. Gosier, Rick Watts and Sgt. Eiland

Me needing a shave and having some of the 1,000 mile stare

Mike West

Tex (W.W. Wilkerson)

Not sure who the guy on the left is, then Rick Watts and J.C. Hines

J.C. Hines

Layne Smith really enjoying his C-rations

Brady and Curly

Me and Arkansas

Me, Brady and West having a C-ration breakfast

Painted up for night patrol. Kneeling: me almost out of the photo to the left, then Tex and Mike West. Standing: Arkansas, J.C. Hines, Woods and David Saint John

Norm Myer

Me and Larry Hulbert

Mac Barber and Lonnie Johnson

Our platoon waiting to get on a CH53

Far left is me leaning on Rick Watts, not sure who has the rifle, then Cowboy, not sure who's behind Cowboy, then J.C. Hines, Brady and Mac Barber giving rabbit ears, Taylor standing behind him and Thompson on the right

Moving our Base Camp to LZ Ross

It was early to mid-July and our battalion switched base camps with the Second Battalion, Seventh Marines so then Ross would be the place we would go for a couple of days of rest every 4 to 6 weeks. LZ Ross was more remote than LZ Baldy, our previous base camp, had been. It was about one-fourth mile across and had only a helicopter landing pad and no runway for fixed wing aircraft. It was small enough that it would get attacked from time to time, with the enemy trying to overrun it. I think one time it partially was. There were some framed in huts with tin roofs for the guys who lived there, which included an artillery battery, re-supply personnel, some corpsmen and a doctor.

Also at LZ Ross was a Navy Chaplain. Sometimes the Chaplains would go out to the jungle to hold a church service, but it never happened while I was with Mike Company. I think the Company Commander didn't want to have a church service in the jungle because we would have to all gather together into a small area, and that would be a bad thing. We were always avoiding getting in groups, because an enemy mortar round or machine gun burst could kill a lot of people in a hurry. The Chaplain held a service while we were there for a two day rest, so I went to a service for the one and only time while I was in Vietnam. I can't remember what the sermon was, but then what does a chaplain say to a bunch of Marines who are trying to kill people every day? I do know I was praying and asking for God's protection and again promising him that if he would get me through this, I WOULD NEVER EVER FORGET.

When Mike Company would spend a couple of days at LZ Ross, we stayed in large tents with bunkers nearby. If I remember correctly, the first time we stayed there I went to the doctor to be treated for diarrhea, which I had been suffering from for almost two weeks. After evaluation of a stool sample of mine, they, it was determined I had hook-worms. The cure was to fast for 12 hours and take some gelatin pills, which were meant to burn the worms out of your intestines. You had to do this for three days in a row, so Mike Company headed out for the jungle without me. I caught up with them after I'd been "wormed" by catching a ride on a re-supply chopper. When I caught up with them, my squad had other squad members taking turns walking point.

The Creek Bed Shootout

Okay Guardian Angel, it's time again

We were on a patrol down in the flat land area and I was third in our squad column. I believe Mike West was at point man and Sergeant Eiland was walking shadow for him. We came upon a steep drop off into a creek bed with a dirt bank about seven feet down and probably an 80 degree slope. At the bottom, it leveled off and went out across a shallow creek. It was roughly 75 feet to the other side where there was heavy underbrush and trees. Mike and Sgt. Eiland had gone down the bank and I was going to try and just slide down the dirt bank and as I started to go down, suddenly a bunch of shots came from over in the bushes on the other side. Mike and Sgt. Eiland hit the deck and I wasn't sure if either of them had been hit. The Viet Cong must not have aimed well, because they missed me, and as my feet hit the creek bed, I lay back against the bank and started shooting back. I couldn't scurry back up the bank, and hitting the deck seemed like it would be a bad move, so I just leaned back against the bank and shot like crazy. Thank goodness those Viet Cong were lousy shots, because from that distance, they should have hit me, or maybe my Guardian Angel had pulled off another good one. With me shooting for about 10 seconds, they stopped shooting. I never did see them hidden in the bushes and trees, and for them to have stopped shooting so quickly, I still wonder to this day, if

I hit one of them. The whole thing only lasted about 15 seconds, but I had learned that in war, a lot can happen in that short of a time.

Mike West and Sgt. Eiland were okay, and like me, couldn't believe that none of us was hit. Sgt. Eiland asked why I just leaned back and shot. I told him it just seemed like the best thing to do at that moment.

The Grenade Duel

It was probably in the same time period, while we were in the flatland area, that one night we had a grenade duel with the enemy. It was maybe 11:00 or 12:00 at night and the VC chucked a bunch of grenades in on us. Someone hollered that we were being attacked. Since they weren't firing their rifles at us there weren't any muzzle flashes to help us determine where they were, so we started throwing grenades back where we thought they were. This went on for a couple of minutes, then everything was over. It turned out that our Squad Leader, J. C. Hine, had been hit and had minor shrapnel wound, but it was decided that we'd hold off on medevac until morning.

When a medevac chopper came in the next morning and J.C. headed over to get on it, Mike West asked "Where's J.C. going?" and we looked at him with a confused look and asked him what he meant. It turned out that Mike had slept through the grenade duel the night before and didn't realize that J.C. had been hit. As I said before, after a while we could get so accustomed to the sound of grenades at night and not wake up.

J.C. was only gone for a day or two to have the shrapnel pulled out and get stitched up, and then he was back.

Trying to Determine Which Civilians were VC Sympathizer's

While we were moving around either as a company or just as a squad on a patrol, we had to try to evaluate whether the civilians we were encountering were on our side or not. Typically, the larger villages with 10 or more thatched huts were favorable to the South Vietnamese government and supported us. Many times, people in these small villages would ask us to stay and live with them for protection from the Communists, mainly the Viet Cong. Villages larger than this were almost always pro South Vietnamese government, wanted our help, and were ready to help us. The small isolated little villages of two or three thatched huts - especially if they were closer to the mountains - seemed to be pro Viet Cong. Sometimes they would act friendly but some were hardcore, and they would be pretty unfriendly. Sometimes we just knew that this mama-san and her kids were the wife and children of a VC soldier, so we had to stay really alert when in these little villages. Sometimes, there would be a thatched hut over to the side, away from the others which seemed to be abandoned. Many times, these would be booby trapped for the un-expecting American who would go looking through them. There's a scene like this in the movie "Platoon" when a guy was groping through just such a hooch. As I watched it, I wanted to shout out "No! Get out of there!", but it was too late, and the booby trap exploded.

Whenever we were in an area that was probably predominantly VC, which was most of the time, we would often go on early morning dawn patrols to get to the little mooches, before papa-san left. A lot of the VC were local, so they would come back at night to see their wife and kids, then sneak out at dawn. Sometimes, we would get there in time to encounter them. I whizzed a few bullets past them as they were high stepping it into the jungle, but they all got away.

I have a lifelong friend - Larry Hulbert, who was with the Second Battalion, Seventh Marines. Larry was a Navy corpsman who volunteered to go on night patrols to sneak up on the little VC villages and catch the VC in the middle of the night. He knew one squad leader who was a real expert in these tactics, and on more than one occasion they caught the VC in the middle of the night.

Don't be sympathetic towards these murderous terrorists, because, that's exactly what they were. They would sneak into villages sympathetic to the South Vietnamese government and murder people in the middle of the night. As I said at the beginning of the book, we had a noble cause, and that was one of our main objectives: - to keep the countryside safe from these Communist murderers.

The NVA Tea Party

I was still on a break from being the squad point man and our squad was on a patrol being led by Arkansas at point. Behind Arkansas were Mike West and J.C. Hines. This would prove to be one of the craziest patrols we ever went on.

I was about four or five men back in our patrol and I didn't see exactly what occurred, but from what I pieced together later, this is what happened: Arkansas, Mike West and J.C. walked into a VC village, where about six or eight NVA and some villagers were sitting around drinking hot tea. These stupid NVA hadn't even assigned anyone to keep a lookout, so we walked right into their tea party. Arkansas didn't recognize them as NVA with their uniforms on, and thought they were South Vietnamese soldiers. As he turned to say something to Mike West, the NVA finally saw them and started scrambling for their AK-47s. All kinds of shooting broke loose and Mike and J.C. nailed three of them right off the bat. The rest of them ran into the jungle. I saw a couple disappear into the underbrush, and sent a few bullets chasing after them. Then my rifle misfired, so I ejected that round, and it misfired again. I didn't know why that happened, but it was a mystery to me what had caused it, and I worried that it could happen again.

So Mike and J.C. had nailed three NVA who were trying to get off some shots after having tea with some locals. Several others escaped into the jungle before we nailed them, so they lucked out.

Since Arkansas was at point and hadn't recognized the NVA as the enemy in a timely fashion, I got my point man job back. It was kind of a mixed emotion to become point man again. I was proud to have such a dangerous job, but any fool could see that the job could get you dead or wounded quicker than the other squad members.

The Death of Sergeant Eiland

Sergeant Eiland was almost finished with his second year tour of Vietnam. He had spent an R&R in Hawaii with his fiancé in the past month and was looking forward to going home and getting married. He had gone to DaNang for his final physical to make sure everything was okay physically for him to go home. Normally after such a trip, he would have spent a few days back at base camp, LZ Ross, and then returned to DaNang to fly to Okinawa. He and the company Gunny had some words about something, however, and Sgt. Eiland went back to the jungles with Mike Company for the last days before going to DaNang to fly home.

It was July 27, 1970 and Sgt. Eiland didn't have to go on any patrols, but he volunteered to go on one, I believe with Bravo Squad. While they were on patrol, we heard a bunch of shooting and later heard over the radio someone was killed in action. Either our Platoon Commander or Company Commander who asked over the radio, "Who was the KIA ?" and the answer came back over the radio, "The KIA was Echo Five Echo," meaning E-5 Eiland. We were all devastated. First, we all liked Sgt. Eiland. But even more painful was to have a comrade and here he was, a guy that was engaged, just a few days from finishing his tour. His getting killed so short from going home was a very demoralizing thing - to know we could be so close to going home and still get killed.

You can find Sergeant Grady Eiland on the Wall at Panel 8W. Line 59

Semper Fi, Marine!

Antennae Valley

Mike Company was given an assignment to go to Antennae Valley to set listening devices along foot trails. This valley was traveled by the enemy bringing supplies and personnel from the Ho Chi Minh trail. Antennae Valley got its name because the enemy notoriously would try to shoot the radio man and his radio, to prevent us from calling in artillery and air strikes. These listening devices we were to set out, could actually sense people walking along the trail, and each device's exact coordinates were known at the artillery base, Firebase Ryder. When we "heard" someone going down the trail, the artillery would barrage those coordinates.

We were sent into this valley for two days and nights, and I was going to need all of God's protection I could get.

We were choppered into the valley in the morning. It didn't take long to see this was not a good place. Just a short distance from where we made our touch down, were the remains of a CH-46 chopper that had been shot down on some previous mission into Antennae Valley. This area was remote and it seldom had American troops patrolling it, so the enemy usually moved around at will. As they saw it, it was their turf and we were trespassers.

We split into platoon sized patrols, each with different locations to go set the listening devices. Alpha Squad was at point for Third Platoon, mainly because J.C. had volunteered us. That made me point for the whole platoon. We were moving in an open area about 200 or 300 feet wide and as you looked out in front of us, it went a few hundred feet. We were coming to a point where another open area was coming up to our left. As we came around to where we could see better in that direction, I saw a group of about eight or ten Viet Cong about 500 feet away. They saw us just before we saw them, and as soon as we were in sight, they started shooting, so I started zipping bullets their direction in response. My first two magazines had tracers every other round, so those went whizzing past them. They then disappeared into the jungle, hoping I'm sure, we would chase them. We weren't going to fall for that ambush set-up, so we just kept going on towards our objective. It was pretty obvious from their boldness, they felt this valley was theirs.

After we had set in the listening devices along the trails, the entire company got back together and found a good location to spend the night. Out in front of our fighting holes was an open area about 120 feet across- then solid jungle.

With the attitude shown by the VC earlier that day, we figured there was a good chance they would attack us that night. Rick Watts was my fighting hole partner, and we dug our hole extra deep. I had a Claymore mine I set out about 110 feet in front of us, just at the edge of the jungle. The Claymore was a command detonated mine that would fire one-eighth inch steel balls by the thousands, in whichever direction it was aimed. The back blast from a Claymore could throw rocks right back at you, so before we fired a Claymore, we were supposed to yell out a warning, so everybody could get down.

That night at 10 PM, 75 percent of us lay down next to our fighting holes to get some sleep and the other 25 percent stayed up on watch. About an hour later all kinds of shooting broke loose. The enemy was around our perimeter about 160 of our 360 degree perimeter. They were directly in front of our position, and muzzle flashes from their rifles were thick and heavy from the jungle 120 feet in front of us.

My first two magazines had tracers every other round, so I was firing red tracers at them and they were firing white and green tracers at us. Either with my first or second magazine, my rifle jammed. Since it was dark, I couldn't see just what the problem was, so I started throwing grenades, since they were in my throwing range. I threw out all my grenades (about four) and then went back to figure out what was causing my rifle jam, and since artillery had finally put some illumination rounds over us, I could see I had a double feed jam and was able to clear it.

All this time, Rick Watts was banging off rounds with his 45 caliber pistol. A couple weeks earlier, as a radioman, he had traded in his M-16 rifle for a 45 pistol to help lighten his load. It was kind of humorous watching Rick standing there shooting the 45 as all the rest of us were blazing away with our rifles.

During all of this shooting, J.C. surprised us all and started shouting out war whoops. But then we thought we might as well, too, so we all joined in. The Viet Cong must have thought we were crazy, but then again, I guess we were.

The shooting had been going on ten or fifteen minutes, with bullets flying everywhere, when I decided to blow my Claymore. When I yelled out, "Blowing the Claymore!" I heard a yell back "No!" in the heat of battle, I yelled out, "Why?!" J.C. yelled back, "Save it in case they try to overrun us!"- I was thinking that blowing the Claymore would take a few of them out and they wouldn't even think about trying to overrun us, but. I followed orders and didn't blow it.

Eventually the firefight started quieting down and finally stopped. We sat there in the silence, and then all kinds of rustling could be heard from the jungle in front of us. We opened up again with all kinds of rifle fire. We got a little fire back, but it didn't last long, and then it was over.

We went on 50 percent watch for the rest of the night, amazed that we had made it without any casualties. I'm certain we had killed and wounded some of them, since we heard quite a bit of rustling around during the lull in the shooting. The VC were known for dragging away their dead and wounded.

The next morning we were talking over what happened the night before. Rick, in his usual humor, said, "I could tell that from the noise being made, with the rustling around after the firefight, that one of them had a 45 pistol slug in him."

I hadn't thought about when I put every other round in my first two magazines that in a night-time firefight, it would appear that I was firing a machine gun. Our machine guns had every fifth round loaded with a tracer .So when the attack was going on, the enemy probably thought I was a machine gunner, and because of that they started concentrating their fire on me and the machine guns. When I was talking to one of the guys in the hole to my right, he said that while I was looking down and trying to clear my jam, he saw a couple of enemy tracers miss me by about a foot. I was glad I hadn't known this at the time and didn't find out until the next morning. With this as just one more close call for me- on an ever growing list of close calls, I was praying even more, asking God to protect me and my buddies. I promised Him that if He would get me through all of this I WOULD NEVER EVER FORGET.

Thinking back on the night before and the possibility of being overrun, I thought about the unwritten and unspoken law. We all knew that if we were attacked with overwhelming forces, the word surrender was not in our vocabulary. If it came to it, we would fight to the death.

We were in Antennae Valley for another day and went out planting the listening devices again. When we dug in that next night in a different location, it was kind of cold and rainy and Rick Watts and I put our ponchos together like a pup tent. The Viet Cong didn't attack that night. I think they had gotten their fill of Mike Company from the night before.

I can't remember the exact chronology as to all of the things happening with Mike Company, but I do remember that shortly after that, Rick Watts got promoted from being our squad Radioman to being the Radioman for Lt. Gosier, our Platoon Commander. Rick and I wouldn't be digging our fighting holes together anymore, but we would still be together in the Third Platoon.

Firefight Cheerleading

When we were inside our company perimeter during the day while other squads were out on patrol, they would at times get in firefights just 200 or 300 yards out from the perimeter. Some-times someone would start cheering on our guys, not that they would ever hear us. But we were showing our support and hoped they were shooting some of the Viet Cong. Guys would yell out "Get 'em! Get em!" At times stray bullets would go whishing past us and we would look at each other, wondering if we should jump into our fighting holes. But no one ever did. We just took our chances and kept cheering. I think back on things like that and know that we really were crazy!

Firebase Ryder

We got a break and were assigned a week's security at Firebase Ryder, which was an artillery base on top of one of the Que Son Mountains. It was similar to our previous duty guarding Firebase Bushwhack where we stayed in one spot for a week, and didn't have to hump 100 pound packs every day to a new perimeter, dig a new fighting hole, and run patrols by day and night. In other words, it was kind of a vacation. Most people would think the living conditions were pretty bad, but then again, they weren't used to the things that we were used to.

At Firebase Ryder, we lived in huts made of artillery ammo boxes filled with dirt and stacked up to about six feet high, a sheet of plywood over the top, and sandbags piled on top of the huts. They were large enough for three or four guys to sleep in each one.

I have a photo showing some of us standing out front of one of these "luxury hotels" complete with our clothesline made of detonation cord. Detonation cord is an explosive cord which we would use to tie several explosives together to set them all off at once. Living at the firebase meant we had to improvise, so we used detonation cord to hang out our laundry.

Part of guarding the firebase included a squad spending two or three days at an outpost about a quarter to half a mile away across the ridgeline from the base. The outpost was to be a stumbling block for the enemy trying to attack the artillery base. Since most obvious direction of attack would be along the ridgeline, the outpost was meant to slow them down. We were grunts and used to being the guys with the dirty jobs.

The outpost didn't have quite as luxurious accommodations as at the firebase. Instead we had a bunker about three feet high, about 10 feet wide, and 20 feet long. It was supposed to hold our entire squad, except for the ones on watch during the night.

Our main job was to make sure none of the enemy came along the ridge-line at night headed for the artillery base for an attack. Our secondary mission, during the day was to, watch out over Antennae Valley, and out across the flatlands to the east towards the ocean, for any enemy activity.

Our first night at the outpost, we heard all kinds of movement in the jungle around us. We chucked a few grenades at the noise. Sometimes it would stop, and other times it wouldn't. We weren't supposed to fire our rifles unless we were fired upon first. We were frustrated because we really wanted to open up with full rifle fire, but we weren't sure if it was the enemy, or possibly Rock Apes. They got their name from the fact that these monkeys would sometimes actually throw rocks. None of us had ever seen any of them, but the sound being made out there wasn't typical of the enemy. The big question was, just what in the world was making all that noise?

The next day, J.C. came up with an idea. He said that he had heard that if you took the flash suppressor off of an M-16, it would sound like an

AK-47. We decided to fake an attack that next night if we heard all that noise out in the jungle again.

When night came, it wasn't too long and we heard a bunch of movement in the jungle around our outpost. We then had a few of the guys unscrew their flash suppressors on their M-16's and start shooting so the command back at the artillery base would think we were under attack from the enemy with AK-47s. The rest of the guys started firing at the noise we had heard in the jungle. We felt firing our rifles was a lot more effective than just tossing grenades.

To this day, we will never know if the noise we heard was the enemy or not, but faking a firefight served two purposes - keeping the enemy away, and helping to entertain a bunch of Marines who were usually itching for a fight.

Itching for a Fight

There were some of us itching for a fight and some that weren't. To a great extent, it depended on how long you had been in the bush fighting the Viet Cong and what your experiences had been. If you had a lot of friends that had been hit in combat or with booby traps, you were looking for some payback. Also, if you had experienced some of the local villagers beg you to protect them from the terrorists that would tend to build up in the back of your mind. You could actually get to a point if a firefight would break out, you had mixed emotions whether to be afraid like anyone would be or look at it as an opportunity to kill some of the enemy. Of course some people are naturally more afraid than others, and you never know until you're there and the bullets start flying, just how you might react.

Humping down from Firebase Ryder

When we had finished our week of vacation at Firebase Ryder, our orders were to load up our packs and start humping down the mountain headed east to the flat lands. The biggest problem was that there wasn't a trail from Ryder down and out of the mountains. Without a trail, it meant blazing our own through triple canopy jungle which was terrible. J.C. had again volunteered our squad to lead the way, which meant I was walking point for all of Mike Company.

The jungle was so thick that I had to have a machete to chop through almost every foot of the way. It was so thick that I would only try to chop a tunnel about five or five and a half feet high, so as I would go through it bending over, my pack and all the stuff attached to it would hang up on all the underbrush and I would have to fight through every foot of this thick stuff. The heat was terrific, and with the heavy underbrush and the other layers of jungle growth, there wasn't any kind of a breeze, so it was pretty unbearable. So what?! Welcome to the life of a Marine Grunt in the jungles of Vietnam. Still, I could only handle two or three hours of this and someone else had to take point and swing the machete.

The jungle was so thick, we couldn't tell where we were. Often someone had to climb up a tree to try and get a fix on our location, not that it really mattered. We spent the night in the thick jungle about half way down the mountains and made it the rest of the way the next day. It was about this time that our Platoon Commander, Lt. Gosier, became the Company Commander when Lt. McAdams year was up and he rotated back to the U.S.

MIKE COMPANY'S WORST DAY OF 1970

I would need some more of God's protection. My Guardian Angel was probably thinking he was getting overworked.

We humped down the mountains to the foothills and sometime in the first day or two, J.C. headed out on an R & R to Hawaii to meet up with his wife. Mike West became the acting Squad Leader until J.C. got back.

The night of August 16, we went on a night patrol to check an area that consisted of a few huts at the base of the hill where we were spending the night. It became obvious that the natives living in these huts were VC sympathizers as we went into one of the huts a woman about 30 years old, started yelling and screaming at us to let everyone in the other huts nearby know we were there. Brady slapped her to shut her up, because otherwise it could have turned into a real nasty situation if her VC friends decided to have a shoot-out with us. Nothing happened, so we proceeded to check out the other huts. Since she had given them plenty of warning, anyone there had disappeared before we got to them. Nothing ended up happening so we went back up the hill to the Mike Company Perimeter to spend the rest of the night.

The next morning another squad went on an early morning patrol back to the same huts where we had been the night before. It was

August 17, 1970 and they encountered the same loud mouthed woman who was obviously a VC sympathizer that we had dealt with the night before. That patrol decided to bring her back to our perimeter and put her on the next re-supply chopper back to DaNang and have her interrogated.

Not long after that patrol returned along with their woman prisoner, some of my friends and I were assigned to set up a landing zone right next to our perimeter for the re-supply choppers that were to be arriving soon. I remember Arkansas was one of the group, but I'm not sure who else was among us. Arkansas was to my left and kind of out in front of me, as we were making a circle around what would be the LZ.

Suddenly our mortar platoon started firing off rounds. I hadn't any idea what they were firing at, but it allowed perfect timing for some VC soldiers to begin firing their mortars at us, since we couldn't hear theirs over our own.

What happened took place a lot faster than I can describe. The enemy mortar rounds started coming in about every two or three seconds. The first round landed about 50 feet in front of Arkansas and both he and I were confused as to what in the world was going on. The second round about three seconds later went off about 30 feet to the right of Arkansas and he hit the ground, I wasn't sure if he had been hit or not. The third round went off about 30 feet to my left. Being the genius that I was, I finally figured out what was going on and dropped to the ground. My fighting hole was a couple of hundred feet away back at the main perimeter, so all I could do was hit the ground and pray no mortars would land right next to me or right on me.

There were about seven or eight more mortar rounds that exploded around us. After they quit coming in, we got up to check out the damage. It was a real mess! The initial count was three dead and twenty-nine wounded. We cancelled the resupply choppers and started calling in medevacs instead.

One of the three killed was Curtis Colyear, the Third Platoon Machine Gun Squad leader. As I had mentioned before, he was from California and I had shot the breeze with him on different occasions and considered him a friend. I didn't know the other two except for their faces.

Colyear's location on the wall: Panel 8W Line 118

Our own squad had suffered three casualties out of all the wounded – Woods, and two new replacements whose names I don't remember. Ron Phroper my Homey from St Joseph, MO, was hit in the lower back, but not fatally. Music from the machine gun squad was hit pretty bad and was unconscious He had that glazed over look in his eyes, which, when a guy looked like that, it usually meant he wasn't going to make it, but I guess he did. Our former Platoon Commander and now the Company Commander Lt. Gosier had been hit in the back of his thigh, but was still walking around trying to keep in command.

With all these dead and wounded, you could smell the blood. I had smelled it before, but this time with this many casualties, the smell was that much stronger, and needless to say, it was nauseating.

Brady only had a couple of weeks left before going home, so I was worried about him. I didn't want another guy who was real short, to get killed like Sgt. Eiland. I was really relieved when, after looking around for him, I found he was okay.

The woman prisoner the squad had just brought from their morning patrol was also killed.

We loaded chopper after chopper with dead and wounded and finally got everybody medevacked. Whoever was in command decided at that point the rest of Mike Company would hump back to Ross about three or four miles away. As we were headed there we were ambushed and took three more wounded. We medevacked them and headed out again for Ross. As dusk fell, the point man for the lead squad hit a booby trap. Three more were wounded. By now it was dark and we had to do a night medevac, dropping aircraft illumination to light things up enough for the medevac chopper to land. We got those three out I thought we would just dig in and spend the night, but the order came we were going to keep heading for Ross.

Having what was left of the company headed for Ross in the dark was a risky proposition. As there were a couple of tanks at Ross, they sent one out to get us and lead us back. By the time we got to LZ Ross, it was almost dawn.

Between the mortar attack, ambush headed for Ross and the booby trap, we had three killed and thirty-five wounded. Two of the wounded died within days, so we lost five that day. Combined Mike Company had been depleted of almost a third of its men, so we were in a rebuilding mode while at Ross. We got some new replacements and even got some guys from re-supply. While we were there, J.C. returned from his R & R from Hawaii.

The locations on The Wall for those five:

Curtis Colyear, Panel 8W Line118
Charlie Taylor, Panel 8W Line 120
Moses Jones, Panel 8W Line 118
Richard Savio, Panel 7W Line 006
John Reese, Panel 7W Line 013

As I said before, Curt Colyear was a friend. The rest of them were familiar faces of fellow Marines struggling through a really tough existence as Grunts in the jungles of Vietnam.

You can go to the Mike Company web site – www.mike37.org - to see them and all of the brave Marines who died fighting with Mike Company.

You can go to the Vietnam War Memorial web site at www.thewall-usa.com and look up any of them for more information and messages left by friends, relatives, and even people who never knew them.

While we were back at LZ Ross, we could go dig out our Sea Bags at the supply hut, which had our personal belongings in them. Some of the guys had transistor radios (remember those things?), and would listen to the military radio station in DaNang. The number one hit in Vietnam for most of the Marines and soldiers was "We Gotta Get Out of This Place" by Eric Burdon and the Animals. The radio station tried to play all kinds of music, and one of the songs I remember was "Everything is Beautiful In Its Own Way" by Ray Stevens. The song starts out with a choir of small Sunday School kids singing "Jesus Loves the Little Children". To hear those sweet innocent voices made me almost remember another world that I used to be part of, in a place far, far away. No one can comprehend what life was like for the Grunts, living pretty much like animals. And when we woke up in the morning and pushed ourselves up off the ground, our main mission for the day was to find the enemy and kill him and to keep ourselves alive.

Another song they would play on the radio was Peter Paul and Mary singing "Five Hundred Miles." which is about someone 500 miles away from home. Ha! Try 10,000 miles! There were, I'm sure, some guys in Vietnam who were living in some kind of real dwelling. They were listening to Peter Paul and Mary and getting homesick and melancholy, so then they would go and have a beer to cry in. The Marine Grunts didn't have that luxury. Maybe it was a blessing in disguise.

We didn't have access to drugs either. We lived in the jungle in constant danger and being impeded by any kind of drugs was a real "no-no," so we didn't have that problem to deal with like some did both in Vietnam and when they came home.

At any rate, Mike Company got patched back together and packed up and headed for the jungles again.

SNIPER VALLEY

We were on patrol one day shortly after we had left LZ Ross and were headed through an area known as Sniper Valley. It's easy to guess how it got its name. It was a valley southwest of Ross a couple of miles that passed between Hill 271 and the foothills of the mountains. Sniper fire would come from both directions, but most of it came from Hill 271.

I was walking point going along a creek to our left, though we couldn't actually see it because of all the trees and bushes. I was coming up to a spot where there was a break in the trees and bushes along the creek. As I got to it and looked to my left, there sitting in the creek bed eating their lunch were four VC about 75 feet away. They hadn't even noticed me and I probably should have aimed in and started shooting. Instead, I pointed my rifle their direction and yelled "Lai Dai!" which means "Come here!" Well I never saw four people grab their rifles and disappear into the jungle so fast! I sent some bullets chasing after them and don't know if I hit any of them, but it apparently didn't take any of them down. We weren't going to chase after them. That would just be asking for them to ambush us.

We kept moving along with our patrol and got to a trail that went up one of the foothills. We followed it for a while. Things were pretty uneventful, so we headed back on the same trail we had come on. Going back the same way was risky business, but we didn't have much choice.

We started taking sniper fire from Hill 271. At first we just got down and started firing back at the snipers, who were hidden in the jungle and probably about 100 yards away. The snipers stopped shooting for a while, so we started moving again, but then the sniping began again. We decided to use a LAAW rocket and fire at the sound of the snipers shots. David St. John proceeded to fire the LAAW and the rocket made its usual big explosion in the general direction of the sniper. We began to move again, and as David St. John would later tell me, three sniper rounds just missed him as they kicked up dirt and water from a rice paddy nearby. These little creeps were real persistent. Finally one of them hit one of our guys in the leg. He was a new replacement and I don't know his name. But now it was time for a medevac, and we would have a hot LZ if we didn't take care of the snipers.

Before we could have the medevac chopper come in, we called in an air strike. An F-4 Phantom jet came swooping in and dropped some napalm, and that was the end of the sniping.

A BAD DAY FOR ALPHA SQUAD

My prayer I said, or at least should have said: "Guardian Angel, you better guide my steps today."

It was about a day or two after Sniper Valley, August 24, 1970. We had already been on two patrols that day when J.C. volunteered us to go on yet another, to scout out a good position for Mike Company to act as a blocking force for a "Sweep and Block Operation" at dawn the next morning. Our new Platoon Commander was a Lieutenant and had just become our leader a week or so before. Again, he was with us such a short time, I don't remember his name but he came along on the patrol.

I was walking point following a foot trail and observed two or three C ration cans laying in the middle of the trail, so I detoured around them about three feet to the left . A little earlier we had seen someone who may have been VC disappear into the trees way out across a rice paddy to our left. I was about 75 feet down the trail when an explosion went off behind me back where the C ration cans were. J.C had hit one of the cans and it had a grenade booby trap underneath it. J.C. was in pretty bad shape and our Platoon Commander had been hit in the chest, but not fatally. We didn't know it at the time, but Mike West had also been hit with a small piece of shrapnel in the back of the neck. We called in a Medevac chopper for J.C. and the Lieutenant. J.C. was unconscious with that glazed look in his eyes and we knew it was bad. He died on the chopper while heading for the hospital. I wasn't sure what had happened – why J.C. hadn't followed my steps – but he may have been distracted by the possible VC we had seen earlier.

As I led the squad back to our perimeter, there was Rick Watts waiting for me. Since he wasn't our Squad Radioman anymore, he didn't go on the patrol and was in the Company perimeter when he heard the explosion from the booby trap. When word came over the radio that we had hit a booby trap and had two wounded, he figured I was one of them. He later heard over the radio that the wounded were J. C. and the Platoon Commander. As I walked up to Rick he said "You never get hit do you? How do you do that?" I told him that I prayed a lot. He said that most of the guys prayed, and I just shrugged my shoulders and said "What can I say?" As I look back on it, I think of how here it is 40 years later and I am still thanking God for protecting me. Maybe my protection came from not just praying while I was there, but also for all the years in the future.

The Platoon Commander would have usually been the one to write the letter to J.C.'s wife, but he had been wounded and medevacked. It was going to be up to the squad to write a letter to Nancy his wife and their little boy. We really weren't sure just what to say, but we did our best to let her know that J.C. was a real good Marine and a great Squad Leader. I remember J.C.'s younger brother was in Marine training and he sent our squad a letter. I found out thirty-nine years later that Mike West had gotten Nancy's address while we were still in Vietnam. He had written her a letter and she had written back. I didn't know Mike had her address, but wish I had known, because for years after I came home I had wanted to send her a letter as well, telling her what a great Marine her husband had been.

There were a lot of long faces in our squad after losing J.C., but we were still in the jungle and had to keep trudging along. Before dawn the next day, I was leading the entire company back to where J.C. had been killed and then past that point a short distance, for us to set in as a blocking force. While I was leading the way and dawn was breaking, I saw a tree branch laying across the trail, so I made a big detour around it to the right. We set in and waited to see if the sweeping force would herd any of the enemy our way. There wasn't much chance of it, since medevacing J.C. the day before, pretty well gave away our position. Nothing happened, so we started back to our company perimeter, On the way, somebody took a closer look at that tree branch across the trail and could see a booby trap trip wire attached to the branch and going over to the left where a grenade was hidden. If someone would have gone around the branch in that direction or moved the branch, it would have set it off. One of our guys tied a cord to the branch, then got way back and pulled it and it set off the booby trap explosion with everyone a safe distance away. It was obvious the area we were in was full of booby traps.

It was after this "Block and Sweep" tactic that day that Mike West told us about the piece of shrapnel he had gotten in the back of his neck, when J.C. had been hit. We called in a medevac chopper to take Mike back to the hospital in DaNang to have the shrapnel pulled out and get stitched up.

J.C. Hines location on The Wall: Panel 7W Line 001

Semper Fi, Marine

Bad News for Bravo Squad

It was August 27, three days after J.C. had been killed and Bravo squad was out on patrol. We heard an explosion in the distance, then heard over the radio that they had hit a booby trap and taken two casualties. One was dead and the other was wounded. Mac (Ernest) Barber had been killed while he was walking point and Taylor had been wounded. Mac and Taylor were both from Alabama. I really liked Mac and the teasing we would do with each other. We had just lost Sgt. Eiland from Alabama a month before. Even though Lynyrd Skynyrd's "Sweet Home Alabama" was recorded after we lost these two Marines, I am sure they are enjoying it in Heaven.

Just how much of this death stuff did we have to take? We were sad enough already from the mortar attack and J.C. getting killed, now we lost Mac Barber. That's seven men killed in ten days. We sure couldn't keep this up. The Grunts had a saying in Vietnam "You've never lived until you've almost died". If you had experienced several close calls, you could kind of add an echo to it "You've never lived until you've almost died, almost died, almost died". I was continuing my talks with God and again promising him that if he would get me through all of this, I WOULD NEVER, EVER FORGET.

Mac's location on the wall: Panel 7W Line 015

A New Platoon Commander

Since our previous Platoon Commander (the Lieutenant whose name I can't recall) was wounded when J.C. was killed, we got a new one. I hate to say it, but I can't tell you the new Platoon Commander's name either. Rick Watts was his radioman and he came to me one evening and said that Recon had spotted some NVA headed our general direction. We were being warned to watch out for a possible attack. Then he kind of chuckled. The new Platoon Commander had asked him who he should have with him when checking the fighting hole positions of the Platoon. That meant he was a little nervous about being in the bush with a potential attack warning. Rick was my biggest fan, so he informed me that he had told the Lieutenant to have me stick close to him in case we were attacked. As Rick was telling me this, he was getting a real good laugh out of it.

Malaria or Not

Nothing happened that night with the enemy, but I had been feeling sick and had a temperature. It finally reached 104 degrees, which meant it was time for a medevac. It appeared I had malaria, because I had cold chills along with the high temperature. It had gone past sunset, so the medevac would have to be the "Big Kahuna," where they dropped aircraft illumination from a cargo plane for the chopper to see while they were landing. I was impressed that they were doing all of this for me, a lowly Lance Corporal. I kept my rifle with me on the medevac, but left all of my ammo behind for my squad members. When the chopper picked me up, we climbed to an altitude of about 10,000 feet, which really felt cold for me with my fever. They finally landed at the First Medical Battalion in DaNang. Before taking me to the hospital, the guys at the landing pad looked through my gear. My flak jacket still had four grenades in the pockets. They just shook their heads, no doubt realizing that we grunts came from a whole different world than they had to deal with.

The hospital at the Marine First Med was kind of a joke. They had us in a framed-in building, the two-by-fours were showing on the inside, and it had bare concrete floors and tin roofs. In any case, even though I had the symptoms of malaria, it turned out I had some kind of parasite. The open sores were what we called jungle rot. Anytime we would get a scratch from a thorn or a bush, or like the sore I had from my cartridge belt rubbing me raw, it would never heal. The constant dampness caused by sweat, wading through rice paddies, and rain kept them from ever drying out and healing. Wading through the rice paddies, rivers and the like, with open sores meant all kinds of nasty stuff could get into your wounds.

I healed up in about a week and then headed back to Mike Company and the jungle. While I was gone, one of the new replacement guys had been given the job as point man. When I got back, they had me give the new point man some lessons and tips on how to walk point, since I was the only guy that anyone could think of that had the job for six months without getting wounded or killed. I tried to give him a crash course on everything I thought would make a difference in keeping him and the rest of the squad alive. I had been proud to be the point man, but I was ready to pass the job on to someone else.

I'M READY FOR R & R

I was eligible for R & R, and a friend I had made in the first platoon, Norm Myer, was also eligible to go at the same time. I'm not sure how we got to be friends, but I know we used to talk about cars all the time. We went to DaNang together and took our physicals, to make sure nothing was wrong with us. I had developed a real problem with my left arm. I had played college football at Northwest Missouri State University for two seasons, playing corner linebacker. I had injured my left shoulder once, when tackling a big fullback during a game. I guess it was that injury in conjunction with carrying 100 pound packs through the jungles of Vietnam that finally took its toll. I told the doctor in DaNang of how I could hardly raise my arm above my head and how my muscle under my arm, the lat, had deteriorated down to nothing. He told me to go ahead on R & R and come back and see him when I got back.

Norm and I ended up getting our R & R's to Bangkok, Thailand and it was terrific. The first couple of days I ate steak three times a day. Steak and eggs for breakfast, steak for lunch then steak dinner in the evening. We finally started eating some of the local Thai food and it was great, too. I had never had authentic oriental food before that, and I still love it today.

I'M MEDEVACED AND THE SEVENTH MARINES GET PULLED OUT

When we got back from R & R I went back to see the doctor and he figured it was beyond his capability to diagnose what was wrong. He wrote up orders for me to catch a medevac flight to Japan on a big cargo plane from the Air Force Base at DaNang. I was supposed to go back to LZ Ross and our Mike Company headquarters and get all of my gear together and get back to the Air Force Base at DaNang. From there I was to check into the Air Force Hospital for the flight to Japan.

I had no idea what was going to happen regarding this medevac to Japan. We had other guys in our squad get medevacked to Japan, then get patched up and sent back to Vietnam a month or two later. As far as I knew, that was what would happen to me.

When I got back to LZ Ross, all of Mike Company was there. The Seventh Regiment had gotten orders to stand down and leave Vietnam for Okinawa. About one third of the guys were actually going to go to Okinawa and the rest were getting re-assigned to other units.

Among the guys going to Okinawa were David Saint John, Tex and Roger Thompson, but it seemed like almost everybody else was getting reassigned. Rick Watts was going to a CUPP unit (Combined Unit Pacification Platoon), where Marines would live in a village and help protect it from the Viet Cong Terrorists with the help of the local civilians. Mike West was getting reassigned to Fox Company, 2nd Battalion of the 9th Marine Regiment. Norm Myers was being reassigned. I'm not sure who I would have been assigned to if I wasn't being medevacked.

While I was with Mike Company our squad had JC killed in action and 13 wounded including the dog. I have to include the dog, because God had him take a bullet for me. The entire company had 13 killed in action and about 150 wounded. For the entire time Mike Company had been in Vietnam, they officially had 161 killed in action and an estimated 1,500 wounded. Our squad had credit for 12 enemies killed and JC was our only killed in action. The overall statistics for Mike Company for the over 5 years they were there, was about a 10 to 1 ratio in the number of the enemy we killed compared to our killed in action.

All of Mike Company got a truck ride from LZ Ross to DaNang, where we went our separate ways. I went to the Air Force Base and checked into the hospital to inquire about catching my medevac flight. Wow! This was a real hospital and was almost like being back in the U.S. It was nothing nearly as rustic as the Marine hospital I had been in earlier for the high fever for the parasite in my bloodstream. That's the way it went in Vietnam. Seems the Marines never got anything as good as the Air Force or the Army.

When we arrived in Japan, they sent the Army medevac patients to an Army hospital and the Marines to the Naval Hospital at Yokosuka. I was put in a hospital ward with about 20 beds in it and the doctors started putting me through a bunch of tests.

Bad News in the Mail

I had been in Japan a few days, when some mail actually caught up with me. There was a letter from Norm Myer and he had written me to let me know Rick Watts had been killed in action October 5. Man, this was terrible news! Rick had been such a close friend; it was devastating to find out he had been killed. All those big times we were going to have together in Florida would never happen. It would be 30 years later that I would find out just how he got killed. Michael Beggs was Rick's Lieutenant and he put an account of it on Rick's site at the Vietnam War Memorial web site. Rick had been shot in the chest while they were on patrol with the CUPP unit. He was killed while he and his fellow Marines were trying to protect Vietnam Villagers. Sadly, it seems that the American people and the rest of the world never heard stories about these kinds of things that took place in Vietnam. Typically only things like the Mi Lai Massacre atrocity with Lieutenant Calley were ever publicized.

I had never gotten Rick's mother's name, thus I never did get a chance to write her to tell her what a great friend and Marine her son had been. About 10 years ago, I was able to make contact with one of Rick's sisters – Isabel Somera – through personal messages left at his site at the Vietnam War Memorial website.

Rick's Location on the Wall: Panel 7W Line 115

Semper Fi, Marine and good friend.

I'm Heading Home

While I was at the Naval Hospital, they decided that I had a torn nerve in my left shoulder, which was something they couldn't fix. This meant I wasn't going back to Vietnam and they sent me to the Naval Hospital in Great Lakes, Illinois, where I received a medical discharge for a permanent disability. My Guardian Angel had done his job and God had done what I had asked for and even more. I had basically prayed that I would come home alive, knowing there was a good chance that I would get wounded, especially as a point man. I learned to never underestimate what prayer can do for you.

Now More Than 40 Memorial Days Have Gone By

If you are in Washington, D.C. and go visit the Vietnam War Memorial and see the names of the over 58,000 men on The Wall, say hello to some old friends of mine.

William "Bill" Taylor Panel 12W Line 37
Sgt. Grady Eiland Panel 8W Line 59
Curtis Colyear Panel 8W Line118
John "J.C." Hines Panel 7W Line 001
Ernest "Mac" Barber Panel 7W Line 015
Rick (Richard) Watts Panel 7W Line 115

All the men who died with Mike Company are listed on the Mike Company web site at Mike37.org. In the five years Mike Company was in Vietnam we lost 161 men.

You will not find my name on the wall--David Leslie Ray and that is one of the reasons you will find me in church every Sunday, praising God and thanking him for all he has done for me and my family all these years. He brought me safely home, and I WILL NEVER, EVER FORGET.

Me, Mike West, and his younger son Mark in the early 1980's

Mike Company reunion 2009. Me, David Saint John, Layne Smith and Mike West

Mike Company Gets Congressional Recognition

In July of 2007 Congressman Lee Terry of Nebraska helped pass a Congressional Resolution H. Res. 541 praising Mike Company of the 3rd Battalion, 7th Marines, 1st Marine Division for their service during the Vietnam War.

The resolution praised the heroic actions of the Marines of Mike Company which was in Vietnam from June of 1965 to late September of 1970. During that time, they lost 161 Marines and Navy Corpsmen who were killed in action. The number of wounded was probably near 1,500.

During the time the resolution was being passed, the Mike 3/7 Vietnam Association was holding their annual reunion, which in 2007 was in Washington D.C. The founders of the association ran into each other at the dedication of the Vietnam War Memorial and have had annual reunions ever since then. At the reunions, a memorial service is held, where each of our fallen comrades' names is read with a ringing of a ship's bell after each name. It can be emotional.

Mike Company's Killed in Action in Vietnam

Name	Date of Casualty	Location on The Wall
Glen King	September 10, 1965	02E Line 080
Miguel Trejo	October 22, 1965	02E Line 131
Fernando Seda	December 25, 1965	04E Line 038
Donald Zobolish	March 1, 1966	05E Line 131
John Williams	March 1, 1966	05 E Line 094
Thomas Fears	March 2, 1966	05E Line 094
Daniel Manzaro	April 1, 1966	06E Line 072
William Johnson	April 1, 1966	06E Line 071
Lynn Smith	April 17, 1966	06E Line 120
Charles Norris	April 21, 1966	06E Line 127
Charles Gurtler	April 21, 1966	06E Line 126
Fredrick Miller	March 1, 1966	06E Line 126
Henry Tisdale	April 21, 1966	06E Line 127
James Hakes Jr.	May 15, 1966	07E Line 061
Billy Caby	July 9, 1966	09E Line 009
Anthony Calverley	July 15, 1966	09E Line 024
Isaiah Wilson	July 15, 1966	09E Line 027
Richard Demers	July 15, 1966	09E Line 023
Robert Croce	July 15, 1966	09E Line 022
Samuel Reed	July 15, 1966	09E Line 025
Thomas McConahy	July 15, 1966	09E Line 025

Casco Howell	July 20, 1966	09E Line 047
James Metoyer	August 31,1966	10E Line 005
James Clark	September 20,1966	10E Line 123
Norman Napierata	September 22, 1966	10E Line 133
Charles Slager	October 18, 1966	11E Line 089
Marion Kempner	November 11, 1966	12E Line 055
Jerry Potts	November 26, 1966	12E Line 122
James Bowens	November 26, 1966	12E Line 119
William Broad	January 27, 1967	14E Line 090
Fred Pederson	January 28, 1967	14E Line 092
Russell Wagner	January 28, 1967	14E Line 93
Jackya Grant	January 28, 1967	14E Line 090
Joe Kelly	January 28, 1967	14E Line092
Pedro Swenson	January 28, 1967	14E Line 092
Robert Keri	February 1, 1967	14E Line 104
Steven Goldsboro	February 8, 1967	15E Line 009
Peter Lullivan	February 8, 1967	15E Line 010
Edgar Odiot	February 15, 1967	15E Line 034
Michael Carter	February 23, 1967	15E Line 078
Mills Miller	March 16, 1967	14E Line 094
Liam Casey	April 2, 1967	17E Line 091
James Nicholson	May 14, 1967	19E Line 121
Don Redfearn	May 17, 1967	20E Line 018
Bobbie Ratliff	June 19, 1967	22E Line 017
Willie Rhodes	June 19, 1967	22E Line 018
Michael Perkins	June 24, 1967	22E Line 059
Thomas Dineen Jr	August 10, 1967	24E Line 098
John Campbell	August 13, 1967	24E Line 107
Larry Campbell	August 19, 1967	25E Line 014
Fiberto Aguirre Jr	August 26, 1967	25E Line 045

John Booth	August 26, 1967	25E Line 046
George Roland	September 5, 1967	26E Line003
David Shoemaker	November 2, 1967	29E Line 012
Gerald Kropidlowski	November 2, 1967	29E Line 011
Glen Bates	November 2, 1967	29E Line 009
James Edinger	November 2, 1967	29E Line 009
Patrick Dearborn	November 2, 1967	29E Line 009
Stephano Fiducioso	November 2, 1967	29E Line 008
Willet Ameldola	November 2, 1967	29E Line 008
Davis Jones	November 2, 1967	29E Line 011
Robert Moore	November 2, 1967	29E Line 012
Dana Pitts	November 2 1967	29E Line 012
Raymond Plumey	November 21, 1967	30E Line 058
Michael Ruane	December 18, 1967	32E Line 019
Dave Bartholomew	December 30, 1967	33E Line 001
James Shaw	February 13, 1968	39E Line 025
Ronald Blacksten	February 13, 1968	39E Line 017
Wayne Spare	February 13, 1968	39E Line 026
George Starks	March 18, 1968	45E Line 031
Marvin Votaw	April 14, 1968	50E Line 002
Melvin Decker	April 27, 1968	52E Line 029
Charles Byrd	May 25, 1968	69W Line 001
William Adams Jr	May 27, 1968	65W Line 003
James Inman	June 16, 1968	56W Line004
Lawrence Johnson	July 5, 1968	53W Line021
Robert Thomas	July 21, 1968	51W Line 028
Christopher Garcia	July 22, 1968	51W Line 031
James Kemin	July 22, 1968	51W Line 031
Jorge Martinez	July 28, 1968	50W Line 027
Billy Wilson	August 17, 1968	48W Line 036

Ronald Donohue	August 23, 1968	47W Line 040
Michael Caley	August 24, 1968	46W Line 001
Donald Simonson	August 29, 1968	45W Line 002
Gary Hall	August 29, 1968	46W Line 059
Donny Campbell	August 30, 1968	45W Line 005
Jimmy Williams	August 30, 1968	45W Line 011
Phillip Tompkins	September 14, 1968	44W Line 060
Edward Daubert	September 21, 1968	43W Line 053
David Henderson Jr	November 4, 1968	39W Line 016
Elton Anderson	November 4, 1968	39W Line 015
Duncan Sleigh	November 6, 1968	39W Line 030
Gerald Peterson	November 6, 1968	39W Line 028
James Timmons	November 6, 1968	39W Line 030
Edward Henry	November 6, 1968	39W Line 027
Gerald Mullin	November 6, 1968	39W Line 028
Rafael Soler	November 6, 1968	39W Line 030
Raymond Skaggs	November 6,1968	39W Line 030
William Gordon	November 6, 1968	39W Line 026
Jimmie Harvin	November 9, 1968	39W Line 040
Timmy Miller	November 24, 1968	38W Line 051
Leslie Boling Jr	December 3, 1968	37W Line 028
Jack Schaffner	December 8, 1968	37W Line 069
Edmund Cudnik	December 27, 1968	36W Line 080
Larry Foster	December 27, 1968	36W Line 080
Steven Wilkerson	December 27, 1968	36W Line 081
Richard Sadick	January 24, 1969	34W Line 072
Ronald Floyd	February 9, 1969	33W Line 093
Adrian Smith	February 23, 1969	31W Line 022
Benny Cowley	February 23, 1969	32W Line 093
Billy Underwood	February 23, 1969	31W Line 027

Calvin Howell Jr	February 23, 1969	31W Line 095
Eugene Garrity, Jr	February 23, 1969	32W Line 097
Freddie Tipton	February 23, 1969	31W Line 027
Jerry Taylor	February 23, 1969	31W Line 026
Lester Weber	February 23, 1969	31W Line029
Norman Harmon	February 23, 1969	31W Line 004
Thomas Crook	February 23, 1969	32W Line 094
Roosevelt Johnson Jr	February 25, 1969	31W Line 050
Ronald Jewell	February 26, 1969	31W Line 068
Ronald Conley	April 9, 1969	27W Line 044
Arlie Milam	April 17, 1969	27W Line 102
John Corwin II	April 17, 1969	27W Line 098
Larry Graham	April 17, 1969	27W Line 099
James Triplett	April 17, 1969	27W Line 104
George Williams Jr	May 15, 1969	24W Line 023
Charles Bear	June 11, 1969	22W Line 018
Daniel McNeil	June 16, 1969	22W Line 059
Edwin Zumwalt	June 16, 1969	22W Line 062
Michael Paddock	June 28, 1969	21W Line 029
Geoffrey Smith	July 20, 1969	20W Line 027
Peter Morka	July 24, 1969	20W Line 040
Thomas Fuller	July 31, 1969	20W Line 080
David Torres	August 2, 1969	20W Line 090
John Bring	August 9, 1969	20W Line 117
Charles LeBosquet	August 21, 1969	19W Line 087
Major Morgan Jr	August 21, 1969	19W Line 088
Charles Parks Jr	August 21, 1969	19W Line 089
David Baker	August 21, 1969	19W Line 084
Michael McAninch	August 28, 1969	18W Line 002
Salum Chard Jr	August 28, 1969	19W Line 127

Marco Fregoso	August 28, 1969	18W Line 001
William Davis Jr	August 28, 1969	19W Line 128
Harold Hysmith	October 16, 1969	17W Line 085
Richard Lear	October 20, 1969	17W Line 097
Charles Gambill	January 18, 1970	14W Line 043
Anthony Hains	February 3, 1970	14W Line 097
Raymond Bragg	February 15, 1970	13W Line 015
Don Scott	April 22, 1970	11W Line 038
Thomas McKinney	April 22, 1970	11W Line 038
Joseph Pogue	April 23, 1970	11W Line 042
David Ellefson	April 25, 1970	11W Line 049
Kenneth Martin	June 15, 1970	9W Line 056
Grady Eiland	July 27, 1970	8W Line 059
Charlie Taylor	August 17, 1970	8W Line 120
Curtis Colyear	August 17, 1970	8W Line 118
Moses Jones	August 17, 1970	8W Line 118
John Hines	August 24, 1970	7W line 001
Richard Savio	August 25, 1970	7W Line 006
John Reese	August 26, 1970	7W Line 013
Ernest Barber	August 27, 1970	7W Line 015
Richard Watts	October 5, 1970	7W Line 115

You know you were a grunt in the Marines or Army when –

You put on clean clothes after taking a shower and it feels so good you just smile.

You crawl into a nice clean comfy bed rather than laying in the dirt and mud and just smile.

You are nice and dry and looking through the window at the rain and just smile.

You are sitting at the table eating real food and just smile.

You are carrying a child on your shoulders and not 100 lbs. of gear and just smile.

You can walk along a trail knowing you are safe, and you just smile.

You may think life is tough, but when you think back on what it once was, you just smile.

GLOSSARY OF WORDS

AK-47- An automatic rifle still used widely today and was the weapon of choice of the Communists in Vietnam.

Ammo – Short for ammunition, usually meaning bullets.

Artillery base – Where a battery of cannons is located.

ARVN – Short for a soldier in the South Vietnamese army (Army of the Republic of Vietnam) They were on our side and were also fighting the Communists.

Bandoliers – A way to carry bullets. It could be a series of pouches with a magazine in each pouch, or it could be a string of machine gun ammo draped over the shoulder.

Career Marine – A Marine who is planning on staying in the Corps as a career.

CH-46 – A large helicopter still used today and has two main top turret blades. CH-53 – A large helicopter still used today and has one main top turret blade.

C-4 – Plastic explosive that comes in bricks and is pliable like putty.

Chicom grenade – A grenade made by the communists and looks like a tin can with a handle attached on one end.

Chopper – Helicopter

Corpsman – A medic for the Marines who would take care of the wounded in the field and have other medical responsibilities.

C-rations – Food eaten in the field and came in a carton with 2 or three cans of different types of food, such as a can of ham and lima beans and can of sliced peaches and a can of crackers. The carton also had an accessory foil pouch that had a small pouch of instant coffee, sugar, and creamer. Also the accessory pouch had a plastic spoon, toilet paper and a 4 pack carton of cigarettes.

DaNang – A large city in the northern part of South Vietnam. It was the headquarters for the 1st Marine Division and had an Air Force base.

Detonation cord – Explosive cord that resembled clothesline cord and was used to tie more than one explosive device together, so they would all detonate at the same time.

F-4 Phantom – A jet fighter/dive bomber used by the Air Force, Navy and Marines.

Firebase – An artillery base with a battery of cannons.

Firefight – A small arms battle of short duration. Usually rifles, machine guns and grenades.

Flak jacket – Body armor for the torso and could usually stop shrapnel, but couldn't stop a bullet.

Grunt – Infantry, usually armed with a rifle or machine gun.

Gunny – Gunnery Sergeant, having three stripes up and two stripes down.

Ho Chi Min Trail – A series of trails in western South Vietnam coming down from North Vietnam, where the North Vietnamese would transport men and supplies to support their fight against the US and the South Vietnamese.

Hooch – A rustic home for the Vietnamese, usually with a dirt or stone floor and a thatched roof and some had clay tile roofs.

Hump – Hike.

LAAW rocket – Land Anti-Tank Assault Weapon which took the place of the bazooka for firing a rocket at armored vehicles or bunkers.

LCPL – Lance Corporal-which is an E-3.

LZ – Landing Zone for helicopters

Magazine – Containers for bullets that for an M16 rifle they held 20 rounds (bullets) and when the bullets were all fired out, the empty magazine would be replaced with a full one.

Mamma San – The nickname Americans gave the Vietnamese mothers.

Marine 1st Med - 1st Medical Battalion kind of like the MASH seen on TV.

Marine Recon – A reconnaissance unit that would sneak around in the jungles, hopefully undetected by the enemy, and gather information about the whereabouts of the enemy.

M60 Machine Gun – A light weight machine gun with a bipod on the end of the barrel. Rambo's preferred weapon.

Medevac – Medical evacuation usually of the wounded and usually done by helicopter.

Mi Lai – The village where the notorious shooting of South Vietnamese civilians by US Army forces took place.

Muzzle flash – The flash out the end of the barrel of a rifle or machine gun, which really isn't to noticeable in the daytime, but is very bright at night.

NVA – Soldiers of the North Vietnamese Army, who were the Communists invading from the north.

Night Patrol – A patrol taking place in the dark of the night.

Papa San – A nickname given by the Americans to mean the father of the Vietnamese family.

Point Man – The man at the front of the line of a patrol or larger unit movement.

Purple Heart – The award given for being wounded or killed.

Que Son Mountains – A string of mountains southwest of DaNang about 30 miles and going south about another 20 miles.

Regiment – Would be comparable to an Army Brigade and is made up of 3 battalions with about 500 infantry in each battalion along with their support personnel.

Rice Paddy – A field that rice is grown in and is flooded with about a foot of water for the rice to grow in.

Rounds – Unit of ammunition. For a rifle it means bullets.

R & R – Rest and Relaxation and usually means leaving the country for places like Hong Kong, Bangkok, Hawaii, Australia or Taipei.

Shrapnel – Metal fragment from an explosion from a grenade, mortar round, artillery shell or bomb.

Semper Fi – Short for the Marine Corps motto "Semper Fidelis", which means "Forever Faithful".

Shadow – The guy who walks right behind the point man and he is looking mainly to the right and left flanks, while the point man is looking for booby traps and looking straight ahead.

SKS – A Chinese rifle that can only fire semi-automatic and has about a 15 inch long attached bayonet.

Stand down – The entire Regiment packing up and moving to a new duty station.

Sweep and block operation – Where one group sets in along a line and is trying to be unobserved by the enemy and another unit spreads out and moves in a sweeping fashion towards the other unit, trying to catch the enemy in the middle.

Trip wire – Something real thin and many times is thin fishing line or real thin wire and is meant to be part of a trap that someone hits, because they can't see it.

Trip flare – Set out in front of our positions just before sunset, and if the enemy tries to sneak up on us, they may accidentally set a flare off alerting us of their presence.

Printed in the United States
By Bookmasters